Ready to go!

IDEAS FOR DRAMA

AUTHOR
Alison Chaplin

EDITOR
Roanne Davis

ASSISTANT EDITOR
Dulcie Booth

SERIES DESIGNER
Anna Oliwa

DESIGNER
Anna Oliwa

ILLUSTRATIONS
Bill Houston

COVER ARTWORK
Andy Parker

Text © 2001 Alison
Chaplin
© 2001 Scholastic Ltd

Designed using Adobe Pagemaker
Published by Scholastic Ltd, Villiers House, Clarendon
Avenue, Leamington Spa, Warwickshire CV32 5PR

67890   4567890

British Library Cataloguing-in-Publication Data
A catalogue record for this book is available from the
British Library.

ISBN 0-439-01779-3

ACKNOWLEDGEMENTS
The Queen's Printer and
Controller of HMSO for
material from the National
Curriculum reproduced under the
terms of HMSO Guidance Note 8.

Every effort has been made to
trace copyright holders and the
publishers apologise for any
inadvertent omissions.

Contents

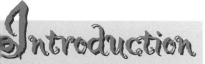

Introduction

Drama is beginning to find an established place in the primary curriculum, within English, and has long been recognized as a subject which benefits the learning and development of young children. There are three main strands to the effective use of drama: a means to build children's confidence and develop their social skills; a teaching approach for exploring cross-curricular subjects and issues; and an aid in developing children's performance and self-presentation skills. These three strands often overlap or interweave, resulting in a learning experience which is productive on many levels simultaneously. Central to all drama work is the concept of 'shared experience', as children learn and work together, and implicit within many lessons is the element of continuous assessment, both of work the children observe and in which they participate. Having the

opportunity to learn through drama provides children with skills, knowledge and understanding that cannot be achieved in the same way with any other subject and that feeds into all other areas of their school and personal lives.

ABOUT THIS BOOK

Many of the activities in this book have been designed to provide both teachers and their children with a simple, yet effective, introduction to a variety of drama methods. The activities have been compiled to develop drama approaches from the simplest games to, finally, making provision for drama in accordance with the revised National Curriculum. The framework for drama in the National Curriculum at Key Stage 1 specifies the range of activities and skills required to ensure effective provision, progression and continuity across the key stages. These are as follows:

RANGE
The range of drama activities should include:
■ working in role
■ presenting drama and stories to others, for example telling a story through tableaux or using a narrator
■ responding to performances.

SKILLS
To participate in a range of drama activities, children should be taught to:
■ use language and actions to convey situations, characters and emotions
■ create and sustain roles individually and when working with others
■ comment constructively on drama they have watched or taken part in.

Many drama activities will focus on more than one of these elements during the same lesson, others will concentrate more on developing the social and personal skills of the children, as specified in the additional English curriculum strands of speaking, listening and group discussion and interaction. All of the activities, however, will develop the children's creative, social or personal skills.

Information on how to organize each activity is designed to be easily adapted for the needs of children of different abilities. Ideas for follow-on work should provide enough material for additional lessons and many of the activities require little or no equipment. This all aims to ensure that teachers, regardless of their experience in teaching drama, can use this book with ease and confidence.

IDEAS FOR DRAMA KEY STAGE 2 (P4 TO 7)
The activities in this follow-up book are arranged under the same headings as those in *Ideas for Drama Key Stage 1 (P1 to 3)*, and provide a built-in progression. Some activities are directly linked, either through content or skills, so you are able to select those most appropriate for the abilities and needs or your children.

At both stages, the activities and drama methods specified can be integrated into a variety of curriculum areas.

INTRODUCTORY WARM-UP GAMES

The activities in this section focus on children:
- getting to know each other
- developing their concentration, observation and memory skills
- learning to respond appropriately to instructions
- interacting positively with others
- gaining confidence
- developing their speaking and listening skills.
  The activities are short. They are not intended to be worked through progressively, and can stand alone as simple games or be delivered as warm-ups at the beginning of a longer session, in conjunction with activities from other sections of this book.

FIND A FRIEND

RESOURCES AND LESSON ORGANIZATION

You will need a medium to large space in which to work. Children work in small groups and then as a whole class.

WHAT TO DO

Ask the children to find a space to stand in and to look carefully at what everyone is wearing. Explain that you want them to form pairs with people who are the same in some way. Tell the children wearing, for example, black shoes to form pairs with other people wearing black shoes as quickly as they can. Any children not matching the criteria should form separate partnerships. Now ask these matching pairs to join up to form groups of four as quickly as possible.

Ask the children to spread out and stand in a space again. On this next turn, impose a time limit countdown from five for the children to form their partnerships, and again to then form matching groups of four. Repeat this complete process with various criteria, for example people wearing white socks, watches, with brown hair, blond hair, blue eyes, wearing glasses.

OBJECTIVES
To enable children to:
- learn each other's names
- work together and form groups
- develop observational skills
- develop memory skills.

CROSS-CURRICULAR LINKS
PSHE
Working co-operatively; following rules; listening to other people.

ENGLISH
Speaking to other people; sounding letters of the alphabet.

Now ask the children to sit down and explain that, this time, they are going to find partners with the same first letter of their name. Ask: *What do we need to know before we can do this?* (We need to know the names of everyone in the class.) Ask each child in turn to call out their first name loudly, advising the rest of the children to listen carefully and remember as many names as they can. Then tell the children to stand in a space again.

Explain that you want them to form pairs with people whose name begins with the same letter as theirs and that, again, you will give a countdown from five as a time limit for this. Any children who have name initials with no matches should form separate pairings. As soon as you have given these instructions, ask: *Are you ready?* and then begin the countdown. Continue as before, with pairs joining together to form corresponding groups of four. Repeat this process several times, with children forming as many different pairs and fours as possible.

Finally, ask the children to reflect on the activity by asking: *Why is it good to play games like this?* (We get to know each other better.) *What does it teach us to do?* (Remember other people's names.) *Why is it important that we get to know each other and remember people's names?* (Because then we can work and play together well and become friends.)

NOW OR LATER

■ Repeat the process with different criteria: eye colour, age, birthday months, surnames, middle names, and so on.
■ Decrease the countdown time limit.
■ Introduce a competitive element by awarding points to the first pair or four formed correctly.
■ Ask the children to mime their initial letters and, in silence, form pairs and groups with others who are performing the same mime.
■ Increase the group sizes as appropriate and according to the different criteria used.

THE SAME AND DIFFERENT

OBJECTIVES

To enable children to:
■ get to know each other
■ follow specific instructions
■ learn to work together
■ develop observational and memory skills.

CROSS-CURRICULAR LINKS
PSHE

Identifying similarities and differences between people; taking part in discussions.

MATHS

Making observations about size and height; using purposeful contexts for measuring.

ENGLISH

Making plans and investigating; sharing ideas.

RESOURCES AND LESSON ORGANIZATION

You will need a medium to large space in which to work. Children work in pairs, small groups and then as a whole class.

WHAT TO DO

Ask the children to stand in spaces and to study the other class members carefully. Explain that today they are going to explore the similarities and differences between each other. Ask: *What is a similarity?* (Something that is like something else.) Tell the children to find a partner with the same hair colour, instructing those children with different hair colour to form separate pairs, and allowing them up to 30 seconds to find partners. Now ask the children to find a partner with the same sized hands as theirs – measuring as carefully as possible. Children with no matching hand sizes should form separate pairs. Allow up to three minutes for the pairs to be formed.

Then tell the children to form additional pairs using further criteria: those who, for example, are the same height, have the same eye colour, the same shoe size *as well as* the same colour hair. Again, any children without matching partners should form separate pairs. Allow an appropriate time limit for each pairing – up to two minutes.

Explain to the children that they have been looking for similarities, things about them that are the same, and then say: *Now I want you to find a partner who is the same as you in one way and different in one way.* (For example, the same eye colour but a different shoe size, or the same hair colour but a different height.) Allow the children up to three minutes to find suitable partners. Repeat this process of finding partners with 'sames' and 'differents' several times, allowing less time for each subsequent pairing.

Finally, ask the children to reflect on the activity by asking: *What have you learned about similarities and differences?* (We all have some similarities and some differences.) *Was it difficult to find people with similarities? Are differences important?* (Some are, but many aren't.) *What could this game teach us?* (That we have more in common with other people than we think and that being different isn't a bad thing.)

NOW OR LATER
■ Repeat the process using different criteria, for example favourite colours, foods, television programmes.
■ Invite the children to suggest alternative criteria.
■ Impose a countdown to create additional tension in the activity.
■ Increase the numbers of similarities and differences to make the task more difficult.
■ Expand group sizes as appropriate and according to the different criteria selected.

PRESENTING MY PARTNER

RESOURCES AND LESSON ORGANIZATION
You will need a small to medium space in which to work. Children work in pairs and then individually within the whole class.

WHAT TO DO
Ask the children each to form a pair with a child they do not know, or do not know well. Explain that they are going to play a game that involves them learning as much as possible about their partner. Tell them that they will each have up to five minutes to ask their partner questions, the responses to which will tell them a lot about the other person. Subjects for questions could include: their name; age; whether they have any siblings; favourite television programme; best holiday; favourite food; favourite subject at school.

Invite the children to make suggestions for questions they could ask in order to discover as much information as possible about their partners. Remind them that they will only have five minutes questioning time each. Now explain that, when they have interviewed each other, you will ask each child to present the information they have found out. Tell them that you will want them to introduce their partner and tell the rest of the class what they have found out through their questions. Advise the children that this means they must listen carefully to what their partners are saying and remember as much of the information given as they can.

OBJECTIVES
To enable children to:
■ get to know each other
■ develop memory skills
■ learn each other's names
■ gain confidence in a group setting.

CROSS-CURRICULAR LINKS
PSHE
Generating a supportive environment; listening to other people; following instructions.

ENGLISH
Developing listening skills; speaking confidently and clearly; asking questions.

7

When all of the children understand what is expected of them, tell them to label themselves 'A' and 'B', and ask the 'A's to question the 'B's first. Move from pair to pair whilst the children are questioning each other, ensuring that they are asking pertinent questions and listening carefully to the answers. Give regular updates on the time remaining and, after five minutes, tell the children to swap roles so that 'B's now question the 'A's.

When the second five minutes of questioning have elapsed, instruct all of the children to stop talking and ask each child in turn (the 'A's first) to introduce their partner, presenting as much information about them as they can remember. Partners should remain silent whilst being presented, only speaking if any of the information is given incorrectly.

Finally, ask the children to reflect on the activity by asking: *Why is it good to play games like this?* (Because we get to know each other better.) *What do we learn from playing it?* (More information about people we didn't know very well.) *Did you find out anything about your partner that surprised or pleased you? Why is it important to get to know each other and remember names?* (To work together better and make new friends.)

NOW OR LATER
- Repeat the activity with children selecting other unfamiliar partners.
- Allow children to write notes whilst asking questions, as in formal interviews.
- Ask the children to write up their interviews before presenting their partners.

GUESS WHO

OBJECTIVES
To enable children to:
- use language effectively
- generate a positive, supportive atmosphere in the classroom
- get to know each other
- follow specific instructions.

CROSS-CURRICULAR LINKS
PSHE
Working co-operatively; taking part in discussions.

ENGLISH
Listening to each other; speaking to different people; speaking with clear diction.

RESOURCES AND LESSON ORGANIZATION
You will need a small to medium work space; a blindfold. Children work together as a whole class.

WHAT TO DO
Ask the children to sit in a circle. Explain that they are going to play a game to see if they can recognize people from the sound of their voice. Advise them that they will have to listen very carefully to play the game well.

Select a volunteer to sit in the centre of the circle, and place the blindfold on them. Tell the other children to get up and silently change places with each other so that they end up sitting back down in a different position in the circle.

Ask the blindfolded child to point towards one of the other children. This child should then say, *Who me?* in their normal voice. Ask the child in the centre to suggest who it is they are pointing at, guessing just by the sound of their voice. If the child guessing finds it difficult to recognize who they are pointing at, ask that child to repeat, *Who me?* up to a maximum of three times.

If they correctly name the person, tell the blindfolded child to remain sitting in the centre, ask all of the other children to change places silently again, and allow the guessing child another turn. Repeat this each time a guesser correctly names the child they are pointing at. If they fail to guess, even after three attempts, ask them to take off the blindfold and swap places with the answering child who then takes a turn in the centre. Again, instruct the children to change positions once the new child has been blindfolded. Repeat the process until at least half of the children have had a turn at guessing.

Finally, ask the children: *Did you enjoy that game? What do you think you might have learned from playing it?* (To control ourselves by being quiet; to listen carefully; to recognize each other.) *How could playing this help you in other areas of your school life?* (It could teach us to be quiet and listen when we are being told something important.)

NOW OR LATER

■ Play the game with children sitting in their classroom places, and the blindfolded child seated or standing at the front of the class.
■ Ask those children pointed at by the guesser to make the task of identification more difficult by using silly voices instead of their own.
■ To make identification easier, ask the child in the centre to make up a complete sentence for the child pointed at to repeat.

PASS THE TAMBOURINE

RESOURCES AND LESSON ORGANIZATION

You will need a small to medium work space; a blindfold; a tambourine. Children work together as a whole class.

WHAT TO DO

Ask the children to sit in a circle. Select a volunteer to sit in the centre of the circle, and then place a blindfold over their eyes. Explain that the rest of the class will now pass the tambourine in turn around the circle behind their backs and that, when you say *Stop!* the child in the middle must point to who they think is holding the tambourine at that point.

Tell the children that you want them to pass the tambourine as quietly as possible and that they must remain silent at all times to enable the guesser to hear any movement of the instrument. Let the guesser know that they will be allowed two guesses per turn and up to three turns to suggest where they think the tambourine is when you call *Stop!*

If the child in the centre guesses correctly by pointing either directly at the child holding the tambourine or extremely close to them, the child holding the tambourine then goes into the middle and is blindfolded and the game begins again. If, however, the guesser fails to point to anyone holding the tambourine in three turns, they should be replaced by a new volunteer. Continue playing the game until as many children as possible have taken a turn in the centre, held or passed the tambourine.

OBJECTIVES

To enable children to:
■ gain confidence in group situations
■ develop concentration skills
■ follow specific instructions.

CROSS-CURRICULAR LINKS

PSHE
Working co-operatively; following rules; developing interpersonal skills; generating a supportive environment.

ENGLISH
Developing listening skills; responding appropriately to others.

PE
Performing actions with co-ordination and control; sending and receiving an object in different ways.

Finally, ask the children: *What do we learn from playing that game?* (How to be silent, how to work together, how to listen carefully, how to be still.)

NOW OR LATER

■ Use different objects or instruments that make a noise, for example a shaker or maraca, a set of bells.
■ Let two different instruments travel around the circle at the same time, asking the child in the centre to listen and point to where each different sound is coming from.

SPOT THE DIFFERENCE

OBJECTIVES

To enable children to:
■ follow specific instructions
■ develop their observational skills
■ develop their memory skills.

CROSS-CURRICULAR LINKS

PSHE

Agreeing to and following rules; taking part in discussions.

ENGLISH

Sustaining concentration; taking turns in speaking.

PE

Performing actions with control and co-ordination.

RESOURCES AND LESSON ORGANIZATION

You will need a small to medium work space; various classroom objects (see 'What to do'). Children work together as a whole class.

WHAT TO DO

With the children sitting in a circle, or their classroom places, tell them to look around the room carefully, noting as many different objects and their positions as possible, because they are going to play a game which will test how observant they are. Explain that you will pick a volunteer, ask everyone to close their eyes and that the volunteer will move an object in the room when no one is looking. When the other children open their eyes again, they have to spot which object in the room has been moved. Now that the children understand what they will be doing, advise them to study the room carefully again.

Select a volunteer and ask this child to stand next to you. Tell all of the other children to close their eyes tightly and bow their heads. Ask your volunteer to walk around the room and to pick up one object and place it in a new position as they go. To provide an additional distraction for the children with their eyes closed, you should also walk around the room, in the opposite direction to the volunteer. (This masks the volunteer's movements slightly and prevents any clever children from listening to the object being moved!) Whilst you are walking around, check that all of the children have their eyes firmly closed and that no one is trying to cheat.

When the object has been moved, return with the volunteer to your original positions and tell the children to open their eyes. Say: *Look around the room carefully and, putting your hands up, tell us which object you think has been moved.* Ask the first child who gives the correct answer to step out and become the next volunteer. Thank the original volunteer and tell them to return to their place.

Play the game again, moving a new object. Repeat the process several times, using different objects and volunteers.

When you have finished playing, ask the children: *Who can remember where all of these objects were originally?* Select two or three volunteers to return the objects to their original positions.

Finally, encourage the children to reflect on the activity by asking: *Did you enjoy playing that game? Why? What do you think it teaches you?* (To be observant about our surroundings; to join in fairly by keeping our eyes closed; to move carefully and quietly.)

NOW OR LATER

■ To assist young or less confident children, move the object yourself into a more obvious new position instead of asking a child to perform the task.
■ Turn the activity into a team game, with points being awarded for each correct answer and teams devising strategies for making the task of guessing more difficult for their opponents.
■ Objects could be added or removed completely instead of simply being moved.

WHO HAS IT?

RESOURCES AND LESSON ORGANIZATION

You will need a small to medium work space; a small object, for example a large button, ping-pong ball or beanbag. Children work together as a whole class.

WHAT TO DO

With the children sitting in a circle, or their classroom places, explain that they are going to play a guessing game which involves them hiding an object from another person, who will try and guess who has it. Select a volunteer and explain that they will be asked to leave the room (or to go where they can't see or hear the rest of the group) and, before re-entering, they must knock or stamp their feet loudly three times as a signal.

Now say that, once the volunteer has left, the rest of the class will pass the object in turn to one another. Then, when they hear the knocking or stamping, whoever is holding the object must hide it quickly on themselves, for example tucking it inside their clothes, concealing it carefully in their hand or putting it in their pocket.

Explain that the volunteer will then be asked to stand in the centre of the circle (or at the front of the class) and must try and guess who has the object. The other children must try very hard not to reveal who is hiding it by avoiding eye contact and keeping their faces impassive. Tell the children that the guesser will be allowed three turns to select who they think has the object hidden on them.

When all of the children understand the process, ask the volunteer to leave and tell them to wait for at least one minute before they knock (or stamp) and re-enter. Now ask the rest of the children to pass the object slowly and carefully to each other. As soon as the first knock is heard, tell the child holding the object to hide it quickly.

When the absent child enters, ask them to stand in their position and guess who has the object. If they fail to do this within their three attempts, ask the child who is holding the object to reveal it. (That child then becomes the next guesser.) If they guess correctly, congratulate them, ask them to sit down, and select a different volunteer to leave the room. Play the game several times, selecting a different volunteer each time.

Finally, ask the children: *Did you enjoy playing that game? Why? What do you think you learned from playing it?* (To listen; to think and react quickly; to keep a straight face; to work together.)

NOW OR LATER

■ Use a password and response instead of knocking or stamping for the 'outsider' to gain entry. This could allow the child hiding the object extra time.

OBJECTIVES

To enable children to:
■ learn how to control facial expressions
■ use hand co-ordination skilfully
■ gain trust in each other
■ react quickly.

CROSS-CURRICULAR LINKS
PSHE
Following rules; taking part in discussions; working co-operatively.

ENGLISH
Sustaining concentration; listening to others.

PE
Sending and receiving an object.

■ Play a musical accompaniment to the game. Pausing it could initiate hiding the object and the re-entry of the guesser.

■ Tie a very small object, such as a button or a bead, onto a circle of string and ask the children to pass this along from hand to hand to the time of an appropriate song. When the singing stops, the outsider comes back to guess who has the object hidden in their hands.

PEOPLE BINGO

OBJECTIVES

To enable children to:
■ get to know each other
■ communicate positively with strangers
■ respond to instructions
■ work within time constraints.

CROSS-CURRICULAR LINKS

PSHE

Working together; following rules; identifying differences.

ENGLISH

Listening to each other; speaking to different people; recording information.

RESOURCES AND LESSON ORGANIZATION

You will need a small to medium work space; one copy per child of photocopiable page 13; writing materials. Children work together as a whole class.

WHAT TO DO

Explain to the children that they are going to play a game of bingo, but that they will fill their bingo cards with the names of other people in the group, rather than cross off numbers. Ask them to look carefully at the different headings in each of the sections on the photocopiable sheet and read these through with them. Tell the children that they must fill each section by writing in the name of someone else in the class who fits the criteria in that section heading.

Tell the children that they cannot write their own name in any of the sections and can only put other children's names on their card once. (No name is to be duplicated.) Advise the children that they must be completely honest about the names that they write in and that those children must match the criteria. Explain that they should find names to write on their bingo cards by looking carefully and asking as many people as possible if they fit the headings.

Tell the children that it is not essential to spell names correctly and let them know that the winner will be the first child to have a different, and relevant, name written in each section of their 'People bingo' card. Explain that you will give them five minutes to get as many names as possible for their bingo cards. When all of the children understand what is expected of them, say: Play 'People bingo'!

Give the children regular time updates, for example Two minutes left, One minute left and so on. This keeps the tension going throughout the game. When the time limit has elapsed, ask the children to stop playing and writing. Find a winner by asking: Who has written a name in every section of their card? If no one has, ask: Does anyone have eight names written on their card? and so on. Some children may complete their cards before the end of the three minutes. Check that the names on any completed cards are valid by corroborating the information with the relevant children. Then congratulate the winner or winners.

Finally, ask the children: Did you enjoy playing that game? What did you learn from it? (We learned names and facts about each other.)

NOW OR LATER

■ Impose a shorter time limit from the beginning of the game, giving children regular updates on how much is remaining for them to complete the task.

■ Add more squares to the bingo card.

■ Change the criteria in the sections. You could include more in-depth, less obvious information, for example about siblings, pets, favourite cartoon characters.

■ Use the same technique for dictionary work: write words in the different sections and ask children to define them.

Name

Date

People bingo card

Someone with black hair	Someone wearing a dress	Someone with blue eyes
Someone wearing white socks	Someone with blond hair	Someone wearing black shoes
Someone with brown eyes	Someone wearing white trainers	Someone who is taller than you

The activities in this section focus on children:
- developing spatial awareness
- gaining awareness of how they use their bodies
- interacting physically with each other
- working together in small and large groups
- understanding how to convey situations in mime
- learning how to use movements expressively.

These activities introduce children to various skills required for expressive improvisation and performance. Initial exercises aim to encourage physical contact and develop basic spatial awareness. The section then develops these skills to address specific drama requirements. In that respect, some of the earlier activities could be combined with later ones to form extended lessons.

STRETCH IT OUT

OBJECTIVES
To enable children to:
- follow specific instructions
- share a physical experience
- discard physical inhibitions.

CROSS-CURRICULAR LINKS
PSHE
Following rules; taking part in discussions; gaining awareness of their bodies.

ENGLISH
Listening to instructions; sharing ideas and experiences; sustaining concentration.

PE
Performing actions with co-ordination and control; using movement imaginatively; developing basic movement skills.

RESOURCES AND LESSON ORGANIZATION
You will need a large work space. Children work together as a whole class.

WHAT TO DO
Tell the children to find a space and lie on the floor. Ask them to curl up as tight as they can, making the smallest shape possible and hold this for a couple of seconds. Now instruct the children to stretch out on the floor, making the longest shape that they can, again holding this position for a couple of seconds. Next, ask the children to curl up their bodies again but this time using a different shape from their first curled position. Tell them to hold for a couple of seconds and then to stretch out, again using a different shape or position to their first stretch.

Repeat this process two or three times, each time asking the children to curl and stretch in different directions. Finish by telling the children to relax and lie flat on the floor again, before all sitting up.

Select three or four children and ask them to show their curl and stretch positions to the rest of the class. Lead a brief discussion with all of the children about how each position made their bodies feel and what different positions they moved into.

NOW OR LATER
- Select suitable music to work to – something slow with an easy-to-follow tune would be ideal.
- Ask the children to suggest different variations of each movement.
- Create a movement routine using all of the different curl and stretch positions.

PARTNER TO PARTNER

RESOURCES AND LESSON ORGANIZATION

You will need a large work space; a whistle; tape or CD player and music to dance to. Children work in pairs and then together as a whole class.

WHAT TO DO

Ask the children to stand at one side of the room. Select one child and ask them to pick a partner. Instruct these two children to skip around the centre of the room together, preferably holding hands. Explain that, when you give the command *Change!* you want the two children skipping together to split up and choose new partners. When this command has been given, the two pairs should then continue skipping around the room with their new partners until you call *Change* again, whereupon they split up and find new partners, forming eight pairs.

Continue calling *Change* until every child in the class is skipping around the room with a partner. If you have an odd number of children in your class, either skip around with the 'spare' child yourself, or allocate them to another pair to form a three. When all of the children are skipping around the room with their partners, call *Change* once or twice more, to encourage children to change partners again. Finally, instruct all of the children to go back to their places – their original position at the side of the room.

This process can be repeated two or three times, giving you the opportunity to select first any children who were not paired at the end of previous turns.

Now explain to the children that you are going to ask them to *dance* in pairs. Let them know that when they hear your *Change!* command (or when you blow your whistle), they must pick a new partner and continue dancing. Play suitable music and select two children to begin dancing to the music in the middle of the room. After a short while, give the *Change* command, instructing these children to select new partners. After a few seconds, repeat the command, and continue in this manner until several pairs are dancing.

At this point, give the command *Everybody dancing!* and instruct all of the children waiting to be selected to join in the dancing in the centre of the room. Allow this dancing to continue for several seconds, or until the end of the music, and then give the instruction *Rest*. This exercise can then be repeated, selecting a different pair of children to begin it.

Thank all of the children for their efforts and lead a brief discussion about how the activity could link into their life at school, how it made them feel and how they think the children waiting to be selected felt.

OBJECTIVES

To enable children to:
■ interact positively with each other
■ make new friends and work with strangers
■ make positive physical contact
■ discard physical inhibitions.

CROSS-CURRICULAR LINKS
PSHE

Following instructions; responding positively to others; generating a supportive environment; working co-operatively.

ENGLISH

Listening with understanding; sharing experiences.

PE

Using movement imaginatively; performing basic movement skills; repeating simple actions.

MUSIC

Listening, responding and moving appropriately.

NOW OR LATER

■ Select appropriate pieces of music to accompany each activity. Many pieces by Sousa would be suitable for the children to skip around to; some of the pop music from the charts would be excellent for the children to dance to.
■ Music with a particular mood could be used as a basis for different types of movement, for example walking slowly, hopping, crawling or running.
■ The same method could be applied to activities based around sequence dancing, country, folk or line dancing.
■ Children could be asked to suggest a sequence of movements to a particular piece of music that the rest of the children copy as they join in.
■ The activity could lead into PSHE work on 'friendship' and 'exclusion'.

FOLLOW THE LEADER

OBJECTIVES

To enable children to:
■ follow instructions
■ work together as a team.

RESOURCES AND LESSON ORGANIZATION

You will need a large work space; a tape or CD player and suitable marching music (for example by Sousa). Children work together as a whole class.

WHAT TO DO

Explain to the children that you are all going to move around the room and that you want them to follow you, copying your movements at all times until you instruct them to rest.

Select an abstract mode of movement, demonstrate this to the children and ask them to follow you in a line around the room, copying your movement as they travel. After a few seconds of moving around the room in this way, change your movement style whilst you are still travelling. The children should copy this new mode of movement. Continue to move around the room, changing your movement regularly, and gradually making it more complex. When you have made several changes and the children have followed you around the room for some considerable time, stop moving and tell them to rest.

Now select a volunteer to act as the leader whom all of the other children will follow. Ask this child to choose a movement method and begin travelling around the room. Instruct the other children to follow this new leader, as before, copying their movements exactly. After a few moments, tell the child leading to change their movement whilst travelling, and instruct the rest of the class to copy the new movement, continuing to follow the leader.

Repeat this process several times with three or four children. Each child should be reminded before they start to change their movement style whilst leading, and the other children should be advised to follow and copy the leader at all times, until they are told to rest.

Now explain to the children that you will lead them again, but that this time they are going to be moving around the room in time with some music. Play a rousing piece of music and begin marching around the room, telling the children to follow and copy you. After a few seconds, stop the music and give the instruction *Rest*. Choose another child to lead the marching and tell the rest of the class to follow and copy them. Ask the leader to stand up straight with head and eyes facing forwards and to swing their arms carefully whilst marching. This should encourage all of the children to copy this marching style. Start the music again and instruct all of the children to follow the leader. After a short while, change the leader and repeat the process.

Finally, encourage the child leading to think about the patterns they are making on the floor with their line of marching children, and ask them to change direction regularly, or to make specific shapes such as zigzags or 'S' patterns. Allow the marching to continue for a few moments longer, and change the leader as often as appropriate. Then ask the children to rest.

Thank them for their efforts and lead a brief discussion, asking them to consider the difficulties in following others, to reflect on the different movement styles used and how they travelled across the floor space. Can they suggest other methods of movement for leaders and followers?

NOW OR LATER

■ Use music in the earlier section of the activity as well, to provide a rhythm for the initial movements.
■ Ask the children to devise their own simple movement routines for others to copy.
■ Try the activity with two or three marching lines going at the same time, moving carefully around the room and weaving in and out of each other without touching or bumping. This gives additional responsibility to the leaders.
■ Refine and polish the marching style until the children are marching effectively in time with the music. Eventually, a simple marching routine could be choreographed, involving the whole class following three or four leaders.

ROBOTS

P_1

RESOURCES AND LESSON ORGANIZATION

You will need: a large work space; a tambour or small drum and beater. Children work together as a whole class.

WHAT TO DO

Ask the children to spread out and stand in spaces. Explain that you want them to imagine that they are robots and ask: *How does a robot move?* (With jerky arm and leg movements in a regimented fashion.) Tell the children: *When I bang my drum (or tambour) I want you to move in time with the beat as if you were a robot.* When all of the children understand what is expected of them, beat a steady rhythm on your drum and encourage them to move around the room as robots. After a short while, stop playing and wait for all of the children to stop moving.

Now say: *This time you must listen carefully to the drum beat and move as robots exactly in time with the beat.* Begin beating the drum in a steady rhythm again then, after a short while, increase the rhythm so that the children move more quickly. After a few more seconds, slow the beat again, continuing to slow it until the children are moving as robots at a very slow walking pace. Continue for a little while longer and then stop beating, waiting for the children to stop moving.

Now explain that you want the children to perform tasks as robots. Ask them *What sort of jobs could we get your robots to do?* (Washing cars, cleaning bedrooms, preparing a meal and so on.) Tell them that, this time, you want each of them to select a task for their robot to do and that they should perform their tasks in time with your drum beat. Take a few moments to ask each child: *What is your robot going to do?* and acknowledge each response, assisting children where necessary.

CROSS-CURRICULAR LINKS
PSHE
Adopting some individual responsibility for the actions of others; generating a supportive environment; following rules; taking part in discussions; setting simple goals.

ENGLISH
Listening to others; making plans; sharing ideas and experiences.

PE
Using movement imaginatively; travelling in different ways.

MUSIC
Responding to music; listening with concentration.

OBJECTIVES
To enable children to:
■ follow instructions
■ use movement expressively
■ work in role
■ use actions to convey character.

CROSS-CURRICULAR
LINKS
PSHE
Working co-operatively;
following rules; taking part in
discussions.

ENGLISH
Listening to and
understanding explanations;
sharing experiences;
sustaining concentration.

PE
Repeating simple actions;
exploring basic ideas; using
simple movement phrases;
travelling; responding to
stimuli.

When all of the children understand what is expected of them, begin beating the drum in a steady rhythm again and move around the room observing and praising children as they perform their tasks in role as robots. Continue for a few seconds and then, again, speed up and slow down the rhythm of the beats, reminding the children to continue performing their tasks in strict time to the beat.

Finally, stop beating and tell the children to sit down. Encourage them to reflect on the activity by asking: *Did you enjoy that? Why? Why not? What was difficult about being robots? What else could you do as robots? Is this acting?* (Yes, because we are being someone or something else.) *How could doing this help us to act?* (We learn to use movements to fit the characters we are being.)

NOW OR LATER
■ Use suggestions from the children for additional tasks to perform as robots.
■ Find appropriate music for the children to move to as robots.
■ Ask the children to form pairs, one child in role as a robot, the other giving them tasks to perform.
■ Invite some of the children to present their work to the rest of the class.

FOLLOW THAT CAR!

OBJECTIVES
To enable children to:
■ follow instructions
■ create roles
■ use actions to convey
characters and situations
■ present drama to others.

RESOURCES AND LESSON ORGANIZATION
You will need a large space in which to work. Children work in small groups and then together as a whole class.

WHAT TO DO
Ask the children each to stand in a space. Explain that you want them to move around the room as different types of vehicles. Ask: *What sort of vehicles could you be?* (Cars, buses, lorries, aeroplanes, ships and so on.) Work through various modes of transport, asking the children to move around the room as each type of vehicle suggested. Allow up to 30 seconds per vehicle.

Now say: *Choose one type of vehicle for yourself. Decide what you are going to be and, when I clap my hands, move around the room as if you are that vehicle.* Check that the children understand by asking a few of them what type of vehicle they are going to be. Encourage as much variety as possible in their choices. When everyone understands what is expected, tell the children to find spaces again. Clap your hands to instruct them to start moving, then, after a short while, tell them to stop.

Now explain that, this time, they are going to move around again as their chosen vehicles but, when you clap your hands, you want them to make a group with other people who are being the same type of vehicle. Advise the children that they can repeat their original vehicle choice or change their movements to a different mode of transport. Reinforce your instructions by saying: *So, all of the cars will go together, all of the aeroplanes will make a group and so on. Anyone who can't find others moving as the same vehicle as them should make a separate group.*

When the children understand what to do, ask them to stand in a space again, and instruct them to begin moving around the room. After a few seconds, clap your hands and allow the children up to a minute to form their vehicle groups.

Once the groups have been formed, explain that you want them to work in their groups and, rather than travelling individually, shape their bodies into one large vehicle. For example, the children in the 'car' group will make the shape of a large car, the children in the 'aeroplane' group will form an aeroplane, and so on.

When the children understand what is expected of them, allow them up to two minutes to create their vehicle shapes. When the time limit has elapsed, ask the children to move their vehicles as a group, so that they move in unison as their type of vehicle. Allow this to continue for up to 30 seconds, encouraging groups to move together slowly and carefully in order to keep their vehicles intact. Ask each group to show their vehicles moving to the rest of the class.

Finally, encourage the children to reflect on the activity by asking questions such as: *Did you find that difficult or easy? What was the most difficult part? What other types of transport could we move as? How could this experience help us with our performing?* (It teaches us to work together and to use our bodies in an imaginative way.)

NOW OR LATER

■ Ask the children to repeat the activity with other modes of transport.
■ Use the process as a basis for 'Follow the leader' (see page 16).
■ Link into projects on 'modes of transport'.
■ The children could research more obscure modes of transport to move as.

(see page 16)

CROSS-CURRICULAR LINKS
PSHE
Following rules; working co-operatively; taking part in discussions.

ENGLISH
Listening to others; sharing experiences; speaking to different people.

PE
Using movement imaginatively; creating movement patterns; expressing and communicating ideas.

CLOTHES RELAY

RESOURCES AND LESSON ORGANIZATION

You will need a large work space; a scarf, pair of gloves, hat and handbag for each team; a chair for each team.

Children work in teams of four to six.

WHAT TO DO

Place the chairs at an equal distance from each other at one end of the room. Put a scarf, hat, pair of gloves and handbag on each chair. Ask the children to form teams of four to six (however the class divides equally) and to line up behind their team members, facing their team chair at the opposite end of the room. Explain that they are going to have a relay race where each member of the team must run to their team chair, put on the scarf, gloves, hat and, carrying the handbag, run back to the team. When they reach their team, the clothes and handbag must be put on (and

OBJECTIVES

To enable children to
■ work co-operatively
■ follow specific instructions
■ develop movement skills.

carried) by the next team member, who runs to the chair, removes the items, places them on the chair and runs back to the team again.

Explain that the next team member in line cannot go until the person in front of them returns and releases them, either by handing over the clothing and handbag, touching their hand, or crossing a specified point or line. Advise the children that they must take time to put the clothes on properly and tell them that any team members not wearing the items in the correct manner will be sent back to the starting line to begin their run again.

Allow the children up to two minutes to discuss tactics, encouraging them to consider the order in which they will run and how they can hand over the clothes items effectively to one another. When the children are all ready, start the relay race, watching carefully for any children not wearing the clothes or carrying the handbag properly.

At the end, congratulate the winning team and, if time permits, allow the children to race again. This enables them to refine their tactics and plan strategies with more precision.

Afterwards, gather the children together and encourage them to think about the game by asking them: *Did you enjoy playing that? Why? Why not? What do you think you learned from taking part in the race?* (To work together; to plan and share ideas; to follow rules; to move quickly and efficiently.) Then ask: *What did (or would) you do differently the next time you raced?* (Take more time to plan properly; use other team members effectively during the handover of the clothes; try not to panic.)

Now or later

■ Add to or reduce the number of items as required.
■ Ask the children to perform a task at each end of the room, for example taking off and putting on shoes; building and dismantling a model.

Space travel

Objectives

To enable children to:
■ respond as themselves in a fictional setting
■ use actions to convey situations and emotions
■ comment constructively on drama in which they have participated.

Resources and lesson organization

You will need a large space in which to work. Children respond individually in a whole-class setting.

What to do

Ask the children to spread out and sit in a space. Explain that they are going to go on an imaginative space journey to another planet and say: *I want you to imagine that you are sitting in a spaceship. Get yourself comfortable in your seat and have a look around you, checking all of your controls and instrument panels. In a moment your spaceship is going to be launched and you are going to land on a new planet. Are you all ready for take-off?* Allow the children a few seconds to adopt their fictional settings and then say: *Your spaceship is ready to go and the countdown begins.* Count down from ten and then say: *We have blast-off!* Encourage the children to react as if they were in a spaceship, reacting to the G-force and working the controls.

Go on to say: *Your spaceship is now travelling smoothly through space and you can look out of the window at all of the other planets. Tell me what you can see out of your window.* Invite several children to describe what they can see through their spaceship windows. Then say: *now your spaceship is going to land on the planet you want to visit.*

Prepare yourself for landing. Ready? Allow the children a few seconds to imagine themselves into the fictional situation. Then count down from five and inform them that their spaceships have landed on their planets.

Tell the children to climb slowly and carefully out of their spaceships, allowing sufficient time for all of them to do this. Ask them to look around at the planet they have landed on and encourage them to describe the planets by saying: *What does your planet look like? Is it a big planet? Is it cold or warm? What is the surface like? What can you see in the distance?* Take responses from as many children as possible, acknowledging and commenting on their descriptions as appropriate. Continue using other prompt questions, such as *Are there any animals on your planet? What do they look like? Can you see any other signs of life? Does your planet have rivers, lakes or seas? Is the surface flat or are there any hills or mountains? What does the ground feel like?* Encourage the children to respond with both actions and verbal answers to each question.

Eventually, tell the children that it is now time to return to Earth. *Climb back inside and get yourself ready for take-off again.* Allow time for the children to mime these actions and then say: *Are you all ready? Have you checked your controls? Prepare yourself for take-off.* After a few more seconds, count down from ten and then say: *We have blast-off!* Finish with the children landing on Earth again and stepping out of their spaceships after their adventure.

Finally, encourage the children to reflect on the lesson by asking them: *Did you enjoy that? What did you enjoy about it? Was it difficult to imagine what your planet looked like? Why? Did any of the other planets sound interesting? Which ones? Why would you like to go there? Could you think of anywhere else we could go in our spaceships? What could we do when we got there? Do you think that you were acting today?* (Yes.) *Why was that acting?* (We were pretending to be somewhere else.) *Could we pretend like this in any other situations?* (Yes, when we make up stories or act in plays and have to pretend we are really there.)

Now or later
■ Ask the children to describe the journey in greater detail, including the inside of their spaceships.
■ Use music to create atmosphere, for example the theme by Richard Strauss from *2001: A Space Odyssey*.
■ Take the children on an imaginary journey as a whole class to visit one planet, describing it as fully as you can and asking them to react.
■ Ask the children to draw or write descriptions of their planets.

Jungle journey

Resources and lesson organization
You will need a large work space; the narrative on photocopiable page 24. Children work together a whole class.

What to do
Ask the children to all stand together at one end of the room. Explain that they are going to make an imaginary journey across the room, saying: *You are all going to pretend that this room has become a jungle. I will tell you about your jungle journey and I want you to act out moving through the jungle.* Explain that their journey will take them across to the other side of the room and that they should listen carefully to your

CROSS-CURRICULAR
LINKS
PSHE
Working co-operatively;
taking part in discussions;
following rules.

ENGLISH
Listening to adults giving
detailed presentations;
sharing experiences;
sustaining concentration;
describing experiences.

commentary, reacting appropriately, using mime (silent actions), to what they hear.

When all of the children understand what is expected of them, begin reading the narrative. Read slowly and pause occasionally to allow the children time to react.

When the children have completed their jungle journey, evaluate the activity by asking: *What was it like being in the jungle? What was the most difficult part of the journey? Why? Were you afraid? What were you afraid of? Did you find it easy to pretend that you were in the jungle? Why? Was that acting?* (Yes, because we were pretending to be somewhere else.) *How could we make our acting more believable?* (By using our faces and bodies more to show where we are, what we are doing and how we feel about the situation.)

NOW OR LATER
■ Use the evaluation to repeat the exercise, encouraging children to be more expressive in their actions.
■ Repeat the journey, but include a threat for the children to react to (from their suggestions).
■ Encourage suggestions for other journeys that they could make, for example across sand dunes, and ask them to mime those.
■ Ask the children to draw or write a description of their jungle journey.
■ Use the exercise to investigate jungle environments and the animals and plants found there.

THE LEAVES

OBJECTIVES
To enable children to:
■ create and sustain roles
■ present drama to others
■ use actions to convey situations, characters and emotions
■ comment constructively on drama in which they have participated.

RESOURCES AND LESSON ORGANIZATION
You will need a large work space; a copy for each child of photocopiable page 25; a chair or piece of gymnastics apparatus (optional). Children work together as a whole class.

WHAT TO DO
Sit with the children in a large circle. Read through 'The Leaves', with the children following. Lead a discussion about what sorts of movements are described in the poem. Suggestions from the children should include: the leaves dancing, floating, scampering, and so on; the moon smiling; the North Wind calling; the leaves whirling and falling to the ground, and so on.

Ask the children to stand and spread out into spaces. Explain that you want them to imagine that they are the leaves and ask them to move around the room with appropriate movements as you read. Read the poem again slowly, to allow the children time to respond, and praise those children making effective or creative movements. When you have read through the poem, ask the children to rest and sit down where they are.

Explain that they are now going to bring the whole poem to life by representing all of the different elements in movement. Select one of the children to represent the moon and invite the other children to suggest where and how this child should be positioned (possibly standing on a chair or piece of apparatus). Select six or seven children to represent the North Wind and, again, lead a brief discussion about their positioning (possibly static at one side of the room, moving amongst the leaves, or travelling from one side of the room to the other). Finally, tell the remaining children that they are to represent the leaves, and discuss with them their positions in relation to the moon and North Wind. (This should include defining their movement area, restricting it to a specified section of the 'performance arena'.)

Once these issues have all been agreed, lead a brief final discussion about what movements the children should use to respond to the poem. For example, the leaves should dance appropriately, the child representing the moon should smile and gesture that they are listening, and the children representing the North Wind should either blow or make other moves to indicate that they are affecting the movement of the leaves.

When these details have been discussed and planned thoroughly, tell the children that you will read the poem through again, and that they are to respond with their appropriate movements as their 'characters' are mentioned. Read 'The Leaves' through again slowly, allowing the children time to respond.

After a complete performance, thank and praise the children for their efforts, ask them to sit in a circle with you again and lead a brief final discussion asking them what they learned from the lesson and how they can use these skills in other areas of their school life.

NOW OR LATER

■ Form older or more confident children into small groups and ask each group to devise and present their own interpretation of the poem, including narrating it themselves.

■ Help the children to use musical instruments to represent the poem in sounds rather than movement.

■ Use musical instruments to accompany the narration and movement of the poem.

■ Ask the children to write their own poems based on complementary subjects, for example autumn, wind, rain and winter. Then go on to use these poems to devise narrated movement performances.

CROSS-CURRICULAR LINKS
PSHE
Working co-operatively; setting simple goals; taking part in discussions; following rules.

ENGLISH
Listening to others; sharing ideas and experiences; sustaining concentration.

Jungle journey

It is a very hot day in the jungle. The sun is beating down, making you tired and thirsty.

You begin walking through the jungle. You walk very slowly and carefully, and look around all the time for dangerous animals that might be hiding in the bushes. You push back a tree branch in your way, holding it carefully in case snakes are coiled in it. You look down at the ground, watching carefully where you put your feet in case of spiders or snakes. The ground is covered with little stones and fallen leaves and you walk slowly to stop yourself from tripping and falling. Suddenly you stop.

A huge tree trunk has fallen down and is blocking your way. You look at it, checking for snakes and other dangerous animals, and then climb over it very carefully. You keep walking, taking a drink of water from your bottle and wiping the sweat off your forehead with your handkerchief. A bird screeching in a treetop above you makes you jump and you look up to see where the noise came from.

You carry on walking, but the path becomes narrower and the jungle bushes gradually get thicker and thicker. You have to push your way through carefully. It gets more and more difficult to keep going, the plants and bushes block the path now and you have to push really hard to get through them. More branches hang in front of your face and each time you push one out of the way, another one comes across from the other side.

You are getting very hot and tired now and you are worried about getting lost. You move very slowly through all of the thick trees and bushes, pushing them out of the way carefully. You keep stopping to look around for dangerous animals and then continue pushing your way through the jungle. Suddenly, the trees and bushes clear and you stop and look.

You wipe your forehead again and take another drink of water. You look carefully into the distance. From where you are standing, you can see the sea. You feel very happy and begin moving more quickly, but still carefully, until you are finally out of the jungle.

The Leaves

The leaves had a wonderful frolic,
They danced to the wind's loud song,
They whirled, and they floated, and scampered,
They circled and flew along.

The moon saw the little leaves dancing,
Each looked like a small brown bird.
The man in the moon smiled and listened,
And this is the song he heard:

The North Wind is calling, is calling,
And we must whirl round and round.
And then when our dancing is ended
We'll make a warm quilt for the ground.

Anon

Section 3 — LANGUAGE AND VOCAL SKILLS

The activities in this section focus on children:
- learning to speak aloud in a group context
- listening to others speak
- providing appropriate verbal responses
- responding to instructions
- using language expressively
- conveying situations, characters and emotions through language and sound.

The basic exercises at the beginning of this section encourage children to speak aloud in a group and prepare them for using language and sound expressively. Some of the activities focus on a whole-class choral approach, whilst others develop individual language skills. Activities from the beginning of the section can be combined with later ones to create longer, more intensive sessions.

SOUND CIRCLE

OBJECTIVES

To enable children to:
- create atmosphere through sound
- use language to convey situations
- explore familiar themes.

CROSS-CURRICULAR LINKS

PSHE

Working co-operatively; following rules; setting simple goals; taking part in discussions; generating a supportive environment.

ENGLISH

Listening to each other; exploring sound patterns; speaking to different people.

MUSIC

Using voices expressively; choosing and organizing sounds; working as a class to create sound patterns.

RESOURCES AND LESSON ORGANIZATION

You will need a small to medium space in which to work. Children work together as a whole class.

WHAT TO DO

Sit with the children in a circle and explain that you are all going to work together on making sounds that express places or objects. Suggest a category to the children, for example farm animals, methods of transport, things found at the seaside or the funfair. Ask each child in turn to make the sound of something in your suggested category. Explain that the 'sounds' can include words, nonsense vocabulary, or phrases, and other children can include or repeat another's sound. When every child has made a sound that meets the criteria of your selected category, repeat the process with a new one.

Now think of another category, but do not reveal this to the children. Make a sound from that category and ask the children to pass that sound around the circle. Each child in turn should, therefore, repeat the sound you made. When the sound has been passed around the circle, ask the children to suggest what it was. When the correct answer has been given, invite the children to guess what category the sound belongs to. Once this too has been guessed correctly, ask each child in turn to make a new sound from that category. This time, emphasize to the children that you want them all to think of new sounds from the category, rather than repeating. Finally, ask the children to suggest different categories for creating sounds. Repeat the process with various categories and sounds.

NOW OR LATER

- Ask the children to copy words or sounds precisely, aiming for accuracy of repetition.
- Ask for volunteers to make one or two particular sound effects for the rest of the class to guess.
- Pass complete phrases around the circle for children to listen carefully to, and copy, the different ways they are spoken.
- Ask the children to repeat a particular word or phrase, but to change the way in which it is said, for example *I don't believe it!* can be spoken using various different tones of voice: shocked, angry, excited, miserable and so on.

ALL TOGETHER

RESOURCES AND LESSON ORGANIZATION

You will need a small to medium space in which to work. Children work together as a whole class.

WHAT TO DO

Stand or sit with the children in a circle. Explain to them that they are going to make sounds all together as a group but that, when you say *Cut!* they are to stop making the sounds immediately. Tell them that they are to make sounds only and must not use actual words.

Begin by asking all of the children to make a *Sshhh* sound and continue this for a few seconds to ensure that everyone is joining in. Give the command *Cut!* and then ask the children to make a whispering sound. When all of the children are making this sound effectively, call out *Cut!* again and then instruct the children to make a hissing sound. Continue and repeat this process, asking the children to make, in turn, a mumbling sound, grumbling sound, groaning, praying, chattering, muttering, roaring and, finally, a shouting sound. After each sound has been made effectively by the whole class, the *Cut* command should be given before the next sound is made.

When the children have made all of the sounds you choose, ask them to repeat each sound by giving them a one-word introduction, for example, *Hissing*, but this time omitting the *Cut* instruction, and moving straight into the next sound with the one-word cue.

Once this process has been worked through effectively, explain that you want them to repeat the exercise, but that you want them then to work backwards. So, when the children reach shouting, you then give them the one-word introduction of *Roaring*, then *Muttering, Chattering, Praying, Groaning, Grumbling, Mumbling, Hissing, Whispering* and, finally, back to the *Sshhh* sound.

Practise this process as many times as necessary until the children are all working together and responding to your one-word cues. When the children have travelled successfully up and down the sound scale at least twice, ask them to repeat the exercise a final time but explain that this time, you want the final 'sound' to be silence. At the appropriate moment, give the children the one-word prompt of *Silence* and ask them to hold this for a few seconds. If they do not successfully achieve silence all together the first time it is attempted, repeat the journey up and down the sound scale until they do.

Finally, thank the children for their efforts and lead a brief discussion, asking them what skills the activity teaches them and how these skills can be applied to other areas of their school life.

NOW OR LATER

■ 'Conduct' the children whilst they are making the sounds, using agreed hand signals to indicate when they should increase or decrease their volume.
■ In advance of the exercise, discuss how to make the various sounds, asking the children to suggest how each sound should be made and what it represents.
■ Select alternative sounds to make by discussing and agreeing these as a whole class.
■ Devise sounds that apply to certain situations, for example, opening presents on Christmas Day, and ask the children to put these together in sequence to create a 'sound picture'.
■ Use a handclap instead of the *Cut* command.
■ Organize the children into small groups and allocate a different sound to each, using appropriate hand signals to cue them in.

OBJECTIVES

To enable children to:
■ follow instructions
■ use language expressively and convey emotions
■ respond in unison.

CROSS-CURRICULAR LINKS

PSHE
Working co-operatively; following rules; listening to other people.

ENGLISH
Sharing experiences; speaking with clear diction and appropriate intonation; sustaining concentration.

SIX OF A KIND

OBJECTIVES
To enable children to:
■ think and react spontaneously
■ follow instructions
■ develop memory skills.

CROSS-CURRICULAR LINKS
PSHE
Working co-operatively; generating a supportive environment; behaving in a fair way; setting simple goals.

ENGLISH
Speaking to different people; listening to each other; organizing what they say.

RESOURCES AND LESSON ORGANIZATION

You will need a small to medium work space; a blindfold; a beanbag; chairs (optional). Children work individually and as a whole class.

WHAT TO DO

Ask the children to sit in a circle, on chairs or on the floor. Select a volunteer to sit in the centre of the circle and blindfold them. This child is now 'it'. Hand the beanbag to one of the children forming the circle. Instruct the children to pass the beanbag slowly around the circle to each other and listen for a 'stop' instruction from the child in the centre. When the child who is 'it' calls out *Stop!* they should then also call out a category. This could be: words beginning with the letter 'p', colours, numbers below 20, girl's names, farm animals, and so on. The child holding the beanbag when *Stop!* is called must then name six items in the specified category. Meanwhile, the beanbag should continue to be passed around the circle.

If the child 'naming six' manages to achieve this before the beanbag reaches them again, they then become the new 'it' and replace the child sitting in the centre. If, however, they fail to give six correct answers before the beanbag makes its journey around the circle and back to them, the child in the centre remains as 'it' for the following turn.

The rest of the class need to be advised to pass the beanbag slowly and fairly whilst the child is trying to name their six items from the specified category. The game can be repeated with a variety of categories, and the child being 'it' can have any number of turns until they are replaced.

When the game has been played four or five times, thank the children for their efforts and lead a brief discussion about what new skills or knowledge it taught them, and how these could be applied to other areas of their school life.

NOW OR LATER

■ Ask the children to suggest categories.
■ Plan the categories in advance and specify them yourself.
■ Use the activity to teach children about other subjects, for example characters in stories, modes of transport and objects found at home.
■ Instead of a child in the centre giving a *Stop* instruction, use music to accompany the beanbag passing. When you stop it, the child holding the beanbag tries to 'name six' in a given category.

OBJECT LESSON

OBJECTIVES
To enable children to:
■ use language effectively
■ respond to instructions
■ gain confidence in a group situation
■ use their imaginations.

RESOURCES AND LESSON ORGANIZATION

You will need a small to medium work space; cards from photocopiable pages 33 and 34. Children work individually within whole-class setting.

WHAT TO DO

Ask the children to sit in a semicircle, or in their classroom places. Select one child to stand or sit at the front of the class, facing the other children. Give this child one of the cards and explain that they must describe the object to the rest of the class, but cannot name it or say what it is used for. Ask them to base the descriptions only on the shape, colour and characteristics of the object. Explain that their aim is to provide such a good description of the object on the card, that the rest of the class can work out or guess what it is.

Allow the child a few seconds to think about and plan what they are going to say and then ask them to describe their object to the class. When the child has finished their description, invite suggestions from the other children as to what the object might be. If possible, aim for the same wording as on the card, although extremely close suggestions should be accepted as correct answers.

When an object has been described and guessed correctly, praise and thank the volunteer and ask the child who made the correct guess to come to the front of the class. Give this child another of the object cards and repeat the process with the new object. Continue until several class members have had a turn at describing the objects.

To finish, encourage the children to reflect on the activity by asking: *Did you enjoy that? Why? Why not? What did you find difficult about it?* (Responses will come mainly from those who found describing the objects a difficult process.) *What do you think that activity teaches you?* (To use our imaginations; to think carefully about what we are saying; to listen and concentrate.)

NOW OR LATER

■ Introduce additional object cards with more difficult suggestions on them.
■ Use the process to describe objects in the room, characters from familiar stories or children in the class (only with groups who have learned to be considerate!).

ANIMAL SOUNDS

RESOURCES AND LESSON ORGANIZATION
You will need a large work space; a card for each child from photocopiable page 35. Children work as a whole class then form small groups.

WHAT TO DO
Ask the children to stand in a space, and tell them that they are going to form groups of people who all have the same animal pictures on their cards. Explain to them: *I want you to make the sound of the animal on your card and then find your group by listening for other people who are making the same sound as you.* Advise the children that they must not use real words or discussion to form their groups, only make the animal sounds. Let them know that you will impose a time limit of one minute for the animal groups to be formed and that the first group to find all their animals will be the winners.

When all of the children understand what is expected of them, ask them to start making their animal sounds. Provide assistance where required. (Some children may have difficulty in deciding what sound a particular animal makes.) Give regular updates on the time remaining and, when that has elapsed, instruct the children to stop.

The first group formed correctly should be declared the winners. If none of the groups are complete, either declare the one with the most correct people as winners, or announce that there are no winners this time. Repeat the exercise two or three times, shuffling and redistributing the animal cards each time and gradually reducing the time limit allowed.

Finally, ask the children: *Did you enjoy that game? What did you enjoy about it? Which was the most difficult animal sound to do? Why? How difficult was it to hear your animal sound? What can we*

CROSS-CURRICULAR LINKS
PSHE
Following rules; meeting challenges; speaking confidently in front of others.

ENGLISH
Develop speaking and listening skills; using descriptive language; increasing vocabulary.

OBJECTIVES
To enable children to:
■ use language to convey characters
■ work in role
■ sustain roles individually
■ develop confidence and reduce inhibitions
■ use language effectively.

learn from playing that game? (That we need to listen carefully to each other; that too much noise makes it difficult to hear; when you act you must do it well so that others can understand you.)

NOW OR LATER

■ Use the same process with other sounds, for example onomatopoeic words such as *Zoom! Bang! Whoosh!*
■ Ask the children to add movements to represent their animals.
■ Repeat the process using movements only.

RAINSTORM

OBJECTIVES

To enable children to:
■ use language and actions to convey situations
■ follow specific instructions
■ present drama
■ respond to performances
■ develop concentration.

CROSS-CURRICULAR LINKS

PSHE

Working co-operatively; setting and achieving simple goals; taking part in discussion.

ENGLISH

Sharing ideas and experiences; sustaining concentration; listening to others.

MUSIC

Creating and repeating sound patterns; using sounds expressively.

RESOURCES AND LESSON ORGANIZATION

You will need a small to medium space in which to work. Children work together as a whole class.

WHAT TO DO

This activity is most effective when performed on hard floors. Stand with the children in a circle and explain that they are going to create a 'rainstorm' which they will hear if they listen carefully to the sounds they will make. Instruct the children to copy any movements and sounds that you make and explain that they should join in one by one around the circle, not beginning a new sound or movement until it is passed on to them by the person on their right. All of the sounds and movements will be passed around the circle continuously until, upon its arrival back to you, it will be changed and the new sound or movement passed on again.

Begin by rubbing the palms of your hands together, and do this continuously. The child on your left should copy and continue this, followed by the child on their left, and so on around the whole of the circle until every child is rubbing their palms together continuously. When the child on your right is rubbing their palms together, wait for one or two seconds and then change to clicking your fingers continuously. The child on your left should also change to clicking their fingers, followed by the child on their left, and so on around the circle again. Check that the children continue making the previous sound until the new one reaches them.

When all of the children are clicking their fingers, pause for a moment and then change your sound–movement to clapping your hands. Again, this should be continued in turn by the child on your left, then on their left and so on around the circle, with other children continuing to click their fingers until the 'clapping hands' reaches them. Follow this with slapping your thighs and, finally, stamping your feet, with all of the children copying and changing in turn.

When every child is stamping their feet, pause for one or two seconds and then repeat the sounds and movements in reverse order, going from stamping feet through slapping thighs, clapping hands, clicking fingers and then back to rubbing palms together again. The final moments should involve a gradual return to complete silence, which should be held for a few seconds.

After the exercise has been completed, thank the children for their efforts and lead a brief discussion about the success of the activity. Did they recognize all of the rainstorm sounds? What other sounds coud they make to represent a rainstorm? Talk about what they have learned from the lesson and if they think they can apply the skills to any other areas of learning.

NOW OR LATER

■ Ask the children to suggest alternative sounds or movements that could create an effective rainstorm.
■ Ask for suggestions of themes for other sound pictures that could be created using the same method. Ask the children to devise and perform these and then discuss their effectiveness.
■ Nominate one of the children to lead the sounds and movements.
■ Discuss and explore alternative weather effects that could be created using this process.
■ Use the activity as a starting point for other work on weather.

SOUND EFFECTS

RESOURCES AND LESSON ORGANIZATION

You will need a small to medium work space; a copy of photocopiable page 36 for each child or pair. Children work together as a whole class and then in small groups.

WHAT TO DO

Sit with the children in a circle. Read through the story yourself first, instructing the children to listen and follow closely as you read. Then ask the children to suggest why some of the words have been highlighted in bold, and what these words might represent. (Sounds.)

Now tell the children that you will read the story again, and instruct them to make each sound effect as it is mentioned in the story. Some time can be taken here to allow the children to practise making each sound effect. Read through the story again, a little more slowly this time to allow the children time to respond with their sound effects. When this has been achieved, organize the children into small groups (dividing the circle into sections) and allocate each group one of the sound effects.

Allow the children a short amount of time to discuss and plan how their sound effect will be produced. Now read through the story again, with each group providing their specified sound effect at the appropriate moment.

When you have completed this accompanied read-through, invite the children to suggest other sound effects that could have been performed whilst the story was being read. These would be based on sounds heard at the seaside, such as the gulls screeching. Acknowledge all responses and select three or four of these suggestions to be included when the story is next read out. Discuss briefly with the children where these sounds might occur in the story, and at which points they should be made whilst the story is being read out loud.

Once these additional sound effects have been discussed and agreed, form the class into smaller groups again and allocate each group one of the sound effects, both old and new, to perform whilst the story is being read. Make sure all of the children are clear about what you want them to do and read the story through again slowly, allowing the children time to perform their sound effects.

Upon successful completion, thank the children for their efforts and lead a brief discussion about how effective the sounds were and what they have learned from taking part in the activity. How might they be able to use these skills in other areas of their school life?

NOW OR LATER

■ Use the same method to provide sound effects for other stories, including those familiar to the children.
■ Ask the children to devise and perform a story using sounds and movement only (no words).
■ Ask groups to write stories that contain sound effects, exchange these stories with other groups and perform them.

OBJECTIVES

To enable children to:
■ act out stories
■ use language and actions to convey situations
■ present drama
■ respond to performances.

CROSS-CURRICULAR LINKS

PSHE

Working co-operatively; following rules and instructions; listening to others.

ENGLISH

Speaking to different people; sustaining concentration; making plans; sharing experiences.

MUSIC

Using voices expressively; creating sound patterns; organizing sounds.

TELEPHONE CONVERSATIONS

OBJECTIVES

To enable children to:
■ work in role
■ use language to convey characters and emotions
■ present drama to others
■ respond to performances.

CROSS-CURRICULAR LINKS

PSHE

Following instructions; listening to others; taking part in discussions.

ENGLISH

Speaking to different people; using language effectively; sustaining concentration.

RESOURCES AND LESSON ORGANIZATION

You will need a small to medium work space; two toy telephones (optional). Children work in pairs and as a whole class.

WHAT TO DO

Ask the children to sit in a circle and, if using a toy telephone, place this in the centre of the circle. Number each child consecutively around the circle, beginning with the first child on your left. When all of the children have been given a number, explain that when their number is called out, they must go to the centre of the circle, answer the telephone and begin a conversation with the imaginary person who has called. Encourage them to convincingly portray what the conversation is about and express themselves effectively, so that the rest of the class can understand what sort of conversation it is.

They should continue talking for at least 30 seconds, until you call out another number, whereupon they replace the receiver (real or imaginary) and return to their place. Then the next member of the group goes into the centre and answers the telephone. This child begins a different conversation, continuing it until number three is called and so on.

Insist on the rest of the class remaining silent whilst children are holding their imaginary telephone conversations. If children struggle to think up conversations, encourage them to imagine that they have been called by one of their friends or a

member of their family. Repeat the exercise several times until children are familiar with the process and feel more comfortable about expressing themselves in front of others.

Then place another telephone in the centre of the circle and call out two numbers at the same time. Instruct these children to hold a telephone conversation with each other, the first number called being the one who initiates the call. Again, allow these conversations to run for several seconds, until two more numbers are called out.

The children in the centre should then end their conversation appropriately, replace their receivers and return to their places so that the next two children can begin their telephone conversation. Repeat the exercise several times with different children.

When the activity has been completed, thank the children for their efforts and lead a brief discussion about what they have learned through taking part in the activity and how the skills and knowledge can be applied to other areas of their life.

NOW OR LATER

■ To make the activity easier for younger children, specify what their conversation should be about, for example one friend asking another over for tea or their grandmother ringing to find out what they want for their birthday.

■ Ask the children to use the process to improvise imaginary conversations between characters from stories.

■ Use the exercise for children to ask advice of someone if they have a problem – a teacher could hold the conversation with them.

■ For more confident children working on the individual conversations, ask them to continue the first child's conversation instead of starting a new one of their own.

Photocopiables

Object cards (1)

toothbrush

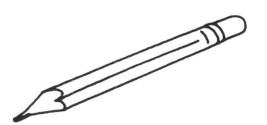

pencil

hairbrush

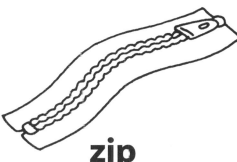

zip

kettle

doorbell

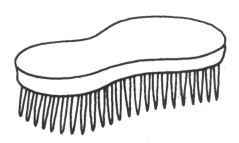

scrubbing brush

step ladder

Object cards (2)

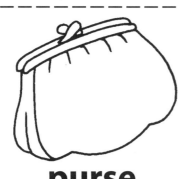

purse

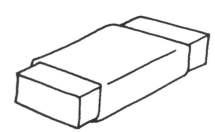

rubber

wellington boot

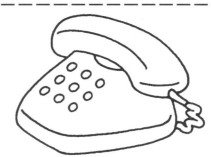

telephone

car

paintbrush

handbag

umbrella

Animal sounds cards

chicken

dog

cat

lion

monkey

pig

Ready to go! IDEAS FOR DRAMA

Matthew's day out

It was a cold and **windy** day when Matthew decided to go for a walk along the beach. The sea was **crashing** onto the sand and the seagulls were flying overhead, making **loud crying noises** as they flew. The **wind** began to blow harder and Matthew pulled his coat tightly around him. His feet made **squelching** noises as he walked across the wet sand and he watched as his wellington boots made footprints that turned into little foot-shaped lakes of water.

As he walked past the clock tower, the big **clock struck** eleven. Matthew began to hurry, walking faster across the **squelchy sand**. He **climbed the stairs** that led to the pavement and **stamped his feet** three times to shake the sand off his boots. Looking around him, he was surprised to see so many people out on such a horrible day.

There were lots of cars on the road, all **zooming** past, and so he walked to the pedestrian crossing, just to be safe. He crossed when he heard the **beeping** sound and began to walk slowly towards his favourite place. He could hear the sounds of **music and screaming** long before he reached it. After a little while he stopped. The music and screaming were even louder now. Suddenly, a man stood in front of him. Matthew looked up, and smiled.

"**Hello, Matthew,**" the man said.

"**Hello, Dad,**" said Matthew. "**Can we go into the funfair now?**"

Matthew's dad smiled and nodded. He took Matthew's hand and they entered the funfair together.

Ready to go! IDEAS FOR DRAMA

DEVELOPING CREATIVE EXPRESSION

The activities in this section focus on children:
- understanding the concept of mime
- responding appropriately to the 'freeze' command
- beginning to concentrate on performance elements
- expressing themselves physically in a creative way
- responding to creative stimuli
- learning how to convey characters, situations and emotions through mime and tableaux.

   This section begins to focus specifically on the skills required for improvisation and performance. The activities at the beginning encourage children to respond creatively to various stimuli, mostly through mime, then develop their abilities using controlled responses in freezes, or tableaux. This provides a sound basis for the activities in the final section of this book.

MOVE TO THE MUSIC

RESOURCES AND LESSON ORGANIZATION
You will need a large work space; a variety of musical instruments, such as a triangle, cymbal, tambourine, bells, drum and appropriate beaters. Children work together as a whole class.

WHAT TO DO
Ask the children to sit in a semicircle in front of you. Tell them to listen carefully as you play each of the instruments in turn and to think of a movement that would suit the tone and timbre of that instrument. Hold a brief discussion of each instrument, inviting the children to suggest appropriate movements. Ask them to give reasons for their choices.

   After this, ask the children to stand in a space and then to move appropriately to each of the instruments as you play them. Advise the children that their movements can either be based on those discussed or be original choices of their own devising. Play each of the instruments in turn (the order should be the same as when originally played) and continue for up to one minute. This ensures that the children sustain each movement for a reasonable period of time.

   When the children have moved to each of the instruments, thank them for their efforts and ask them to rest. Then repeat the process of playing the instruments for the children to move to, but this time, play them in an abstract order, changing regularly to ensure that the children are focusing on listening carefully to the sounds.

   When they have made their more random movements successfully, ask the children to 'freeze' (make still and silent pictures) and then to rest. Lead a brief discussion, asking for comments on the different ways of moving. Which was the most difficult instrument to move to and why? What skills do they think the activity has taught them?

NOW OR LATER
- Select children to play the instruments.
- Ask some children to show their methods of movement to the rest of the class.
- Tell the children to change their methods of movement each time a new instrument is played.
- Use the activity to devise a simple movement or dance piece, with the children working in small groups to create a whole-class performance.

OBJECTIVES
To enable children to:
- follow specific instructions
- develop self-confidence and creative skills
- use actions effectively
- respond to drama.

CROSS-CURRICULAR LINKS
PSHE
Working co-operatively; taking part in discussions; setting and achieving simple goals.

ENGLISH
Listening to others; sustaining concentration; sharing experiences.

MUSIC
Expressing ideas; listening with concentration; exploring musical ideas.

■ Organize older or more confident children into small groups and ask them to devise their own short movement or dance piece based around two or three of the instruments.
■ Use the instrument sounds to create movements that represent emotions, for example fear, anger and happiness, or character traits, such as shy, nasty and friendly.
■ Take the idea a stage further by selecting a familiar story and using a different instrument to represent each character. This could also lead into work on 'Peter and the Wolf', for example.

HAND DANCING

OBJECTIVES
To enable children to:
■ develop creative responses
■ build self-confidence
■ use actions to convey emotions
■ respond to performances.

RESOURCES AND LESSON ORGANIZATION
You will need a small to medium work space; tape or CD player; a recording of 'In the Hall of the Mountain King' from the *Peer Gynt* suite by Grieg (or alternative of your choice). Children work together as a whole class.

WHAT TO DO
With the children in their classroom places or in spaces in the hall, play 'In the Hall of the Mountain King' (or your chosen piece) and tell the children to listen to it carefully. Lead a brief discussion afterwards, inviting the children to suggest what sort of mood

the music invokes, how the tempo differs throughout the piece and how the volume alters. After this discussion, tell the children that you will play the piece of music again and that, this time, you want them to express the mood, tempo, pitch and dynamics of the music with abstract dance movements with their hands.

Play the piece through again. Now lead another discussion, asking the children to suggest specific hand movements that could represent each section of the music. Explore in greater detail the previous elements, also including a discussion about the texture, key changes and overall structure of the music.

Organize the children into small groups and ask each group to devise hand dancing movements to represent different sections of the music: from the quiet, slow passages at the beginning, through key changes, increases in volume and tempo and finally to the loud, fast finale. Allow several minutes for discussion and planning. Ensure that all of the groups

CROSS-CURRICULAR LINKS
PSHE
Following instructions; working co-operatively; taking part in discussions.

ENGLISH
Listening to others; speaking to different people; sharing experiences.

MUSIC
Listening with concentration; internalizing sounds; expressing feelings about music.

are clear about which section of music their hand dances are to represent, and then play the piece again, instructing the groups in turn to accompany the music with their appropriate abstract hand dancing movements.

Finally, thank the children for their efforts and lead a brief discussion on what they enjoyed or found difficult about their performances, what they have learned from the lesson and how they could apply these skills to other areas of their school life.

NOW OR LATER
■ Introduce more specific hand movements to be performed in time with the music. For example, representations of animals, waving goodbye, conducting.
■ Select different types of music to encourage different types of hand dancing movements.
■ In a larger space, ask the children to lay on their backs and to dance with their legs instead of their hands. Use the same process of musical interpretation to devise the leg movements, for example running, moving slowly, circling and scissors.

- When the children gain confidence, ask them to devise their own hand or leg dance movements, without prior discussion. They could then go on to plan a sequence for hands or legs, or both, as a complete routine.
- In a large space, ask the children to dance with their hands and legs in unison.

MIME ORCHESTRA

RESOURCES AND LESSON ORGANIZATION

You will need: a small to medium work space; board or flip chart; tape or CD player; recording of, for example, 'The March of the Toreadors' from *Carmen* by Bizet. Children work in small groups and together as a whole class.

WHAT TO DO

Ask the children to sit in a circle or in their classroom places. Lead a discussion, inviting the children to name the different instruments that can be found in an orchestra. As a memory aid, write the names of these suggestions up on the board.

Select three or four of the instruments and for each one, ask the children to mime the actions of someone playing that instrument. Refine and improve each mime by advising the children to consider such details as pushing the piano pedals, using fingering on the violin strings, pressing valves on trumpets and so on. Ask them also to consider details like turning the pages of their music, watching the conductor and breathing into their instruments. When the children have performed an appropriate mime for each of your selected instruments, explain that they are now going to perform a complete orchestra in mime.

Arrange the class into several small groups, each group representing a different section of the orchestra – strings, brass, woodwind, percussion and so on. Ask the children in turn to present the mimes of their instruments. Praise their efforts and help them to refine their mimes as before.

Now play a suitable piece of orchestral or band music, such as 'The March of the Toreadors', and ask the children to listen carefully for the various instruments being played. When the children have listened to the music, lead a brief discussion about the instruments they could hear and use this information to make any changes or improvements to their mimes.

Finally, play the piece again and tell the children to mime playing their instruments in time with the music as they listen to it. Work through the whole piece, with the children listening and performing their instrument mimes until the end. After one performance, the children may appreciate the opportunity to refine their mimes further. If so, allow them a brief additional discussion and practice period before playing the music again for them to accompany with their mimes.

After a second performance, thank the children for their efforts and recap on the lesson. Ask: *What have you learned from the lesson? Did you enjoy the music? How accurate were their mimes? How could this knowledge be applied to other areas of their school life?*

NOW OR LATER

- For younger or less able children, act as a conductor, bringing in the various groups as a prompt to their performances.

OBJECTIVES

To enable children to:
- develop positive interaction
- use actions creatively
- respond to performances
- work in role.

CROSS-CURRICULAR LINKS
PSHE
Working co-operatively; following rules and instructions; setting and achieving simple goals.

ENGLISH
Listening with understanding; speaking to others; making plans and sharing experiences.

MUSIC
Using movement to express musical ideas; listening with concentration; performing with others; identifying instruments.

- Ask an older or confident child to conduct the orchestra, cueing in the various instrument groups at the appropriate time.
- Select a different piece of music and repeat the process.
- In a large space, ask the children to move around with their instruments in time with the music.
- Use the activity for further work on musical instruments and orchestras.

PASS THE MIME

OBJECTIVES

To enable children to:
- present drama to others
- work in role
- use actions to convey situations
- comment constructively on drama in which they have participated.

RESOURCES AND LESSON ORGANIZATION

You will need a small to medium space in which to work. Children work together as a whole class.

WHAT TO DO

Sit with the children in a circle. Explain that you are going to play a game which is similar to 'Chinese whispers', except that a mime will be passed on instead of words. Ask all of the children to close their eyes and tell them to keep them closed until they feel a tap on their shoulder, when they should open them (and keep them open). Explain that, when tapped, the children will be shown a simple mime which they should then pass on to their neighbour by tapping and showing it to them.

Begin the activity by tapping the shoulder of the child sitting on your left. Show them a simple mime, for example eating an apple, opening a present or writing a letter. Instruct this child to then pass this mime on to the child sitting on their left by tapping their shoulder and showing them the mime. The mime should be passed on in this manner all the way around the circle.

Make sure the children know that they must not open their eyes until they are tapped, and cannot request a second showing of the mime; they should simply pass on what they think they have seen or what they can remember. Continue all around the circle, with the final child showing the mime to the rest of the group. Then perform the original mime, showing the children what you passed on to the first child.

Discuss how much the mime has changed and invite the children to suggest why they think it has changed. (Care should be taken during this discussion to ensure that children do not see it as an opportunity to criticize other class members unfairly.) Repeat the exercise several times, ultimately aiming to finish with exactly the same mime as you started with.

Finally, thank and praise the children for their efforts and lead a brief discussion about the skills they have learned during the activity and what else these skills could be used for.

CROSS-CURRICULAR LINKS

PSHE
Working co-operatively; taking part in discussions; setting and achieving simple goals.

ENGLISH
Listening to adults; sharing experiences; sustaining concentration.

NOW OR LATER

- Children who may find it difficult to keep their eyes closed could sit with their backs to the centre of the circle and turn around when tapped.
- Ask one of the children to begin the mime.
- Select mimes with a particular theme, for example foods; making and building things; work and play.

WHAT'S IN THE BOX?

RESOURCES AND LESSON ORGANIZATION
You will need a small to medium space in which to work. Children work together as a whole class.

WHAT TO DO
Sit with the children in a circle. Explain that you are going to perform a mime and that the children must watch carefully. Begin by miming a box; define the size and shape carefully. Ask the children to tell you what it is that you have just mimed. Now mime opening the box, taking care to show how it is sealed, using tape, ribbons, string, and so on and, again, ask the children to explain your mime. Now react to what is inside the box and carefully take it out. This could be any object or item of your choice, for example a furry kitten, a jar of sweets, a snake, a birthday cake, a beautiful silk scarf. Your reactions need to demonstrate clearly what you have found inside your box. Ask the children to suggest what the item is. When they have guessed correctly, put the item back into your box (taking care to mime this appropriately), seal it again if necessary and put the box to one side.

Now explain to the children that they are going to open their own imaginary boxes. Select a volunteer and ask them to perform the mime of examining their box, opening it and taking out an object. Advise this child to help the others to guess what is in their box by reacting well to what they find. When the volunteer has removed their item from their box, and reacted to it, invite the other children to guess what has been found. Praise correct answers and the child who performed the mime. Invite another volunteer to open an imaginary box, repeating the careful mime process and asking the other children to guess what was in the box.

Now tell the children that everyone is going to be asked in turn to open an imaginary box and react to the imaginary object inside. Allow the children a few seconds to decide what will be inside each of their imaginary boxes. Then select a child to begin. Ask them to pick up their imaginary box from the centre of the circle, open it and mime what is inside. Advise the children to take their mimes slowly, paying as much attention to detail as they can. Continue this process around the circle until everyone has opened a box and the others have guessed correctly what was inside. (NB. Some children, due to lack of confidence, will repeat what others have found in their box. It is best to make no comment as taking part even on this level will help to build their skills and self-esteem.)

Praise each child in turn and, when everyone has completed the exercise, thank all of the children for their efforts. Lead a brief discussion about what the children enjoyed and may have found difficult. What have they learned during the lesson? How could these skills be applied in other lessons?

NOW OR LATER
■ Insist on complete silence during the activity, except for when the children are guessing. This adds tension and focus.
■ Specify the objects the children should find in their boxes, to direct their reactions.
■ Ask the children to describe an object verbally, but not name it, and then pass the box to another child, who should mime finding that object or item in the box

OBJECTIVES
To enable children to:
■ develop basic mime skills
■ work in role
■ use actions to convey characters
■ respond to performances.

CROSS-CURRICULAR LINKS
PSHE
Working co-operatively; following rules; taking part in discussions.

ENGLISH
Listening to adults; sharing ideas and experiences; speaking to different people.

Ready to go! IDEAS FOR DRAMA

■ Ask the children to reinforce their mimes by describing their objects in words after performing them. This could also be useful if the other children are struggling to guess the object.
■ Use the activity as a basis for a piece of creative writing about opening a box.
■ Rather than objects, ask the children to mime finding events or occasions in their boxes and to mime how these make them feel.

HAPPY FACE, SAD FACE

OBJECTIVES
To enable children to:
■ develop creative expression
■ use actions to convey emotions
■ work in role
■ create and sustain roles individually
■ present drama to others.

CROSS-CURRICULAR LINKS
PSHE
Developing confidence; understanding emotions; taking part in discussions.

ENGLISH
Listening to adults; sharing ideas and experiences; sustaining concentration.

RESOURCES AND LESSON ORGANIZATION
You will need a medium to large work space; the narrative on photocopiable page 46. Children work individually within the whole class.

WHAT TO DO
Ask the children to stand in a space. Explain that you will read them a story in which certain things happen to a girl. Tell them: *I want you to react as she would to what happens; so if something sad happens, you should have a sad face and if something good happens, you must show a happy face.* Advise the children to use their bodies as well to reflect the emotions they are expressing, and to hold their 'happy' or 'sad' positions until the mood changes.

Ensure that the children understand what is expected of them and then begin to read slowly through the narrative. Walk around the room whilst reading, encouraging and praising children as appropriate. When you have finished reading, select several children to show either their 'happy' or 'sad' faces to the others. Ask the others: *Why have I asked these children to show their faces?* (Because they performed them well.)

Encourage the children to reflect further on the activity by asking: *Why do we need to be able to act happy or sad?* (When we act as other characters, we need to show how they feel.) *Do we act with just our voices?* (No; with our faces and bodies as well.) *How can we make our acting better?* (By thinking hard about our role and really pretending to be that person, by using our own experiences to express feelings.)

NOW OR LATER
■ After evaluation, ask the children to repeat the activity, with small groups showing each other their 'happy' or 'sad' faces. Use this for further constructive discussion.
■ Use the same process with familiar stories, asking the children to respond to events, as specific characters, with appropriate facial expressions.
■ Ask the children to create their own short narratives and to present them in small groups using a combination of narrators and performers.

PARTNER MIME

OBJECTIVES
To enable children to:
■ use actions to convey situations
■ work in role
■ develop mime skills
■ comment constructively on drama in which they have participated.

RESOURCES AND LESSON ORGANIZATION
You will need a large space in which to work. Children work together in pairs, then take part in a whole-class discussion.

WHAT TO DO
Ask the children to find a partner and to stand in a space. (For a class with an odd number of children, a group of three may be included.) Explain that they are going to perform mimes of different tasks or activities and that they must work together well to ensure that their mimes are effective and realistic. They should try to perform their movements in unison, which will mean that they have to concentrate hard at all times. Let them know that the whole class will perform their mimes at the same time

and that you will allow only a few seconds for planning and preparation, making their responses almost spontaneous.

When all of the children understand what is expected of them, ask them to perform the following mimes with their partners, allowing up to 20 seconds for a brief planning discussion beforehand. Subjects for the mimes should include: building a brick wall; playing football; washing a car; throwing and catching a ball; baking a cake; juggling; carrying a long ladder; and alternatives or additions of your choice.

When each pair has performed their mimes, instruct all the children to sit in a circle. Encourage them to reflect on the activity by asking: *Did you enjoy that? Why? Why not? Which mime did you find the most difficult to perform?* (This will probably be 'carrying the ladder'.) *Why do you think that was the most difficult mime?* (We had to plan our movements carefully and keep the length and shape of the ladder the same all the way through.) *What do you think doing this activity teaches you?* (To work well with others; to make our movements realistic; to think about how we perform mimes; to concentrate.)

NOW OR LATER

■ Invite the children to suggest other mimes to be performed with their partners.
■ Ask some of the pairs to show their mimes to the rest of the class.
■ Repeat the activity with larger groups of up to six, suggesting appropriate mimes.
■ Invite children to mime other tasks or activities, with the rest of the class guessing what they are miming.

MOVING ANIMALS

RESOURCES AND LESSON ORGANIZATION
You will need a large space in which to work. Children work in groups, then as a whole class.

WHAT TO DO
Ask the children to form groups of four to six and to stand in a space. Explain that you are going to give them the name of an animal and that you want them to work with their groups to form the shape of that animal and then move it across the room. Advise the children that they should form their animal shapes carefully, making them both recognizable and easy to move. Explain that you will allow up to two minutes preparation time, after which each group will be asked to move their animals in turn whilst the rest of the class observes.

When all of the children understand what is expected of them, ask them to form and move animals from the following suggestions (or your own alternatives): dog, kangaroo, elephant, giraffe, snake, dragon. Check on the groups' progress during the preparation time, before asking each group in turn to show how their animal moves.

CROSS-CURRICULAR LINKS
PSHE
Working co-operatively; taking part in discussions; gaining self-confidence.

ENGLISH
Sharing ideas and experiences; sustaining concentration; speaking to different people.

OBJECTIVES
To enable children to:
■ use actions to convey characters
■ work in role
■ present drama to others
■ comment constructively on drama in which they have participated
■ comment constructively on drama they have observed.

CROSS-CURRICULAR LINKS
PSHE
Working co-operatively; listening to other people; setting and achieving simple goals; making plans as a group; taking part in discussions.

ENGLISH
Sharing ideas and experiences; speaking to other people.

PE
Using movement imaginatively; creating movement patterns; travelling in different ways; expressing ideas.

Repeat the activity with different animals and, when all of the groups have created and moved at least two from your list, ask the children to sit in a circle. Encourage them to reflect on the activity by asking: *Did you enjoy that? What did you find difficult about moving your animals?* (Answers should include keeping the movements together.) *Which was the most difficult animal to move? Which was the easiest? Why do you think that was? What do you think doing that activity teaches you?* (To work and move together; to plan movements carefully; to use our imaginations; to use movements creatively and effectively.)

NOW OR LATER
- Invite the children to suggest other animals to create and move.
- Link the animals to other current topics, for example minibeasts.
- Use the same process for creating and moving methods of transport.

PICTURE FREEZES

OBJECTIVES
To enable children to:
- understand the concept of freezes or tableaux.
- present drama to others
- use actions to convey situations, characters and emotions
- create roles when working with others
- comment constructively on drama in which they have participated.

RESOURCES AND LESSON ORGANIZATION
You will need a large space in which to work. Children work in small groups and then as a whole class.

WHAT TO DO
Tell the children that they are going to create some 'freezes', or freeze pictures. (These can also be referred to as 'still images' or 'tableaux'.) Explain that freezes are completely still and silent pictures that show a scene and looks just as if someone had taken a photograph.

Ask the children to form groups of five and tell them to create a freeze of people sitting around a table eating a meal. Allow up to 30 seconds preparation time, then give a countdown from ten, ending with the command to freeze. View each picture, commenting positively on those that are imaginatively or realistically constructed. Insist that all the children remain still and silent. When you have seen each freeze, tell the children to relax.

Then instruct the children, in the same groups, to create a freeze of children buying sweets in a shop. Again, allow up to 30 seconds for preparation and role allocation, then give the same countdown and *Freeze.* View all of the freezes.

Ask the children to form new groups of six and tell them to create a freeze that shows 'Christmas morning'. This time, allow up to two minutes for preparation. Give the countdown from ten and the freeze instruction, moving around the room to view each freeze in turn. (Children may want to view each other's freezes and this picture would be an appropriate one to show.)

Finally, in the same groups, instruct the children to create a freeze of 'the birthday party', allowing up to two minutes for preparation and role allocation. (You may need to assist with inter-group 'negotiations' as a number of children will want the role of 'birthday girl or boy'!) Give the countdown from ten and the freeze command. View each of the freezes and then invite each group to show theirs to the rest of the class.

Encourage the children to reflect on their work by asking: *What did you learn from taking part in that activity?* (To be controlled, still and silent; to create realistic pictures; to work together.) *How good did you feel you were at freezing? Which picture was the most difficult one to do? Why do you think that was?* Go on to develop the discussion

CROSS-CURRICULAR LINKS
PSHE
Working co-operatively; following rules; listening to other people; taking part in discussions.

ENGLISH
Sharing ideas and experiences; speaking to other people; making plans as a group.

by asking: *How else could you use freezes?* (To depict scenes from familiar stories; to show events from history; to create scenes from original story ideas.)

NOW OR LATER

■ Ask the children to create 'before' and 'after' picture freezes of the scenes used above to give three sequential images. For example, preparing the meal, eating the meal and after the meal; Christmas Eve, Christmas Morning and Boxing Day.
■ Invite suggestions from the children for other freezes and create these.
■ Ask the children to create a picture freeze for the rest of the class to describe and guess the context.
■ Use a series of picture freezes to tell a simple story in sequence.
■ Play an appropriate piece of music and ask the children to create freezes to represent it.

MY DAY

RESOURCES AND LESSON ORGANIZATION

You will need a large work space; the narrative on photocopiable page 47. Children work individually within a whole-class context.

WHAT TO DO

Ask the children to spread out and stand in a space. Explain that they are going to act out a story using mime and freezes. Say to them: *I am going to read a story about the sort of things we all do during the day and I want you to act out the story.* Tell them that the story is entitled 'My day' and describes the sort of things we do during the day, from getting up in the morning to going to bed at night. Explain your instructions: *I will tell you to either 'mime' the actions, or 'freeze' in the position of one of the actions by saying either 'mime' or 'freeze'. If I say 'mime' you must perform the story using actions only, no sound or words; if I say 'freeze' you must freeze in a position that shows what is happening in that part of the story.*

When all of the children understand what you want them to do, read through the narrative slowly, giving instructions as suggested. Allow the children sufficient time to respond and repeat sections if necessary. Move around the room whilst reading, viewing the performances and praising and encouraging children where appropriate.

When you have finished reading, ask the children to sit down and encourage them to reflect on the activity by asking if they enjoyed doing it and what they liked about it. *Was it acting?* (Yes, because we were pretending to be in a different situation.) *Do you think you acted well? How could doing this sort of activity make us act better?* (It teaches us to respond quickly; we have to pretend to be somewhere else; we don't have words to be able to act with, only our faces and bodies).

NOW OR LATER

■ Invite the children to provide ideas for additional narratives, drawing from their own experiences.
■ Ask the children to form small groups and to mime specific aspects of 'their day'.
■ Organize the children into small groups and allocate each a different section of the day to perform in mime or freezes. View these in sequence.
■ Repeat the process using characters from familiar stories, with the children imagining what a typical day might be like for them.

OBJECTIVES

To enable children to:
■ develop their mime and freeze skills
■ respond in role to create stories
■ use actions to convey characters, situations and emotions
■ create and sustain roles
■ comment constructively on drama in which they have participated.

CROSS-CURRICULAR LINKS
PSHE

Working co-operatively; setting and achieving simple goals; following rules; gaining self-confidence.

ENGLISH

Listening to adults; speaking to different people; sharing ideas and experiences.

Ready to go! IDEAS FOR DRAMA

Name   Date

Happy face, sad face

It was the school holidays and one day when Susan woke up, it was raining. She was upset because she wouldn't get to go to the park now. Then her mum said, "I know – let's go swimming instead."

Susan was pleased. She loved going swimming. "Can Lai Ling come, too?" she asked her mum.

"Of course," Susan's mum replied. "Give her a call." But Lai Ling couldn't come, she had to visit her aunty.

"Oh, well, it's just you and me, then," said Mum.

Susan packed her swimming kit and, by the time they were ready to leave, she felt quite pleased that it was going to be just the two of them.

"We'll walk to the baths today," said Susan's mum.

"But it's raining!" wailed Susan.

"A little bit of water won't hurt you. You're going to get wet, anyway."

Susan laughed and they set off for the swimming baths.

The rain had made big puddles and Susan had a lovely time splashing through them all on the way. Her wellington boots kept her feet nice and dry. Suddenly, as they were walking, a big lorry drove through a huge puddle in the road, splashing them both with dirty rainwater as it drove off. "Yeuck!" exclaimed Susan. "It's made me all wet and dirty!"

Susan's mum wiped the water off their faces, muttering "Some drivers shouldn't be allowed on the roads."

"It's all right," said Susan, "most of it went on my coat." And she continued splashing happily through the puddles all the way to the baths.

When they arrived at the swimming baths, the pool was very crowded. "Oh, dear," said Susan's mum. "There's a lot of people in here today."

Susan felt a bit upset to see the pool so full, until she noticed two of her friends in the crowd. "There's Meena and Rachel," she said happily, and waved frantically at them. Eventually Meena and Rachel noticed Susan and swam over to where she stood.

"You coming in?" they asked.

"Yeah," said Susan and dragged her mum off to the changing rooms.

Susan and her mum had a lovely time swimming. The water was nice and warm and all of them had lots of fun together.

On the way home, the rain had stopped and the sun was beginning to peek through the clouds. "What are we having for lunch, Mum?" asked Susan. "All that exercise has made me really hungry."

"I thought I'd make you a nice bowl of soup," replied Mum, adding, as Susan pulled a face, "followed by a huge bowl of chocolate ice-cream."

"Yum!" said Susan happily. It was turning out to be a very good day indeed.

My day

My day begins when I wake up, rub my eyes and stretch my body *(mime)*. I wash my face *(mime)* and get dressed *(mime)*. Then I have my breakfast *(freeze)*, brush my teeth *(mime)* and set off for school *(freeze)*.

At school, I work very hard all morning *(mime)* and then I go out to play with my friends *(freeze)*. I have my dinner *(freeze)* and then work hard again all afternoon, always putting my hand up to answer the questions from the teacher *(mime)*.

After school, I watch some television *(freeze)* and then have my tea *(mime)*. Sometimes I do my homework after tea *(mime)*, but usually I play for a while, go on the computer, or read a book *(mime)*.

I watch a bit more television *(freeze)* and then get ready for bed. I have a bath *(freeze)*, clean my teeth *(mime)*, get undressed *(mime)* and go to bed *(mime)*. Sometimes I read before going to sleep *(freeze)* and when I get tired, I yawn and stretch *(mime)* and then snuggle down to sleep *(mime)*.

The activities in this section focus on children:
- understanding the basics of character work
- creating and sustaining roles
- exploring well-known and unfamiliar characters
- experiencing creative performance
- presenting drama to others
- creating stories.

These activities bring together the work covered in the previous sections. They focus primarily on the aspects of drama associated with working in role, improvisation, performance and presentation, allowing the children more opportunity for constructive assessment of their own work and that of others.

CHARACTER MIME

OBJECTIVES

To enable children to:
- work in role
- use actions to convey character
- develop basic characterization skills
- create roles individually
- comment constructively on drama in which they have participated.

CROSS-CURRICULAR LINKS

PSHE

Gaining self-confidence; setting and achieving simple goals; taking part in discussions.

ENGLISH

Listening to adults; sharing ideas; speaking to other people.

PE

Using movement imaginatively.

RESOURCES AND LESSON ORGANIZATION

You will need a large space in which to work. Children work individually and as a whole class.

P2/3

WHAT TO DO

Ask the children to stand in a space. Tell them that they are going to move around the room as different types of character. Explain that these characters all have jobs or occupations which mean that they move in a particular way. Select one character at a time from the following list: postman, police officer, goalkeeper, soldier, clown, ballet dancer, jockey, tennis player. After selecting and calling out the name of a character, ask the children to mime walking around the room as if they were that character. Comment positively on effective mimes.

Allow each mime to run for at least 30 seconds. Ask the children: *What other character types could you mime?* (Actor, athlete, burglar, cowboy, astronaut and so on.) Select characters from those suggested by the children and ask them to mime moving around the room as those types of people.

Now ask the children to stand in a space again and explain that some characters perform their occupations in one space. Tell the children that you are going to read out some more characters and you want them to mime, in their spaces, how these characters would move. Select and call out one character at a time from this list (or your own): hairdresser, chef, doctor, teacher, pilot. Then ask the children for further suggestions, for example boxer, bricklayer, dentist, secretary. Again, choose a few for the children to mime.

Finally, say that it should be easy to tell what a character does or who a character is just by the way they move. Ask: *Why is this important?* (It helps the audience to know who we are playing when we are performing.) Remind the children: *Acting isn't just about saying words, it needs to include the whole body.* Go on to ask: *Which characters were difficult to mime? Why? Which characters did you feel you mimed well?* Encourage the children to reflect on the creative skills they have gained from this exercise and how they could be used in other subjects. (For example, in better understanding and miming characters from stories, historical figures, people in traditional tales and fables.)

NOW OR LATER

- Invite the children to suggest other character types and use their suggestions as a basis for further work.

■ Suggest an environment, such as a supermarket or restaurant and invite the children to suggest characters who may be present. Use these to create a whole-class mimed scene.
■ Invite individual children to show their mimes to the rest of the class.
■ Use the same activity to mime familiar story characters with specific jobs or occupations.
■ Ask the children to form pairs and to mime two characters performing the same occupation. Invite several pairs to show their mimes to the rest of the group.

HATS!

RESOURCES AND LESSON ORGANIZATION

You will need a large work space; a selection of hats or forms of headwear, such as bowler hat, police officer's helmet, 'wedding' hat, headscarf, flat cap, beret, soldier's cap, baseball cap, bobble hat, veil. Children work individually and then in pairs.

WHAT TO DO

Show the children each of the hats in turn, asking each time: *What sort of person might wear a hat like this? How would they move?* Tell the children that they are going to move around the room in the manner of the person who wears each hat. Ask them to stand in a space and explain that, when you hold a hat in the air, they are to move around the room in the style of the character who would wear that hat. Advise the children to keep an eye out for when the hat you are holding changes. Allow each movement session to last for at least 30 seconds and comment positively on children who are moving in character effectively.

When the children have moved around the room in the style of each hat wearer, ask them: *What other types of people wear hats or items of headwear?* (Miners, builders, judges, chefs and so on.) Select some people from those suggested and, calling out each one in turn, ask the children to mime appropriate movements for those characters.

Tell the children that they are now going to act out scenes between the characters who wear these different hats and other people who might be in a situation with them. Ask the children to find a partner and to name themselves 'A' and 'B'. Explain that, when you hold up one of the hats, those who are 'A's will act as the person who wears that hat and 'B's will act as someone speaking to them. For example, if 'A' is acting as a police officer, 'B' could act as a burglar, a victim of a crime or someone asking directions. Remind the children that they can use dialogue, but should remember to reflect their characters with their movements as well.

Allow the children a few seconds to prepare each scene if necessary and ensure that they all understand what roles they are playing. After a short while performing, tell the children to swap roles, instructing 'B's to act as the 'hat character' and A's as someone speaking to them. Swapped scenes can be in the same context as the original or changed completely. Repeat this for each hat selected, encouraging the children to devise original ideas for their characters. Nominate some partnerships with interesting scenes to show them to the rest of the class.

Finally, encourage the children to reflect on their work by asking: *What do you think you learned from that activity?* Tell them that they have been improvising – acting out characters. Go on to ask: *How could you improve your performances? Which was the most difficult hat to build a character around? Why?* Invite them to suggest how this activity could benefit other areas of their work. (Devising, creating and sustaining characters; performing scripted plays; compiling costumes for characters and so on.)

OBJECTIVES

To enable children to:
■ follow instructions
■ develop basic improvisation skills
■ create and sustain roles individually and when working with others
■ use language and actions to convey characters.

CROSS-CURRICULAR LINKS
PSHE
Working co-operatively; listening to other people; developing self-confidence; achieving goals.

ENGLISH
Speaking to different people; making plans; sharing ideas and experiences; sustaining concentration.

NOW OR LATER

■ Select one hat and build a more complex improvisation around it, asking the children to improvise the characters involved.

■ Ask the children to form small groups, allocate each group a hat and ask them to create a short improvised play based on the character wearing the hat.

INSTANT IMPROV!

OBJECTIVES

To enable children to:
■ develop spontaneous improvisation skills
■ respond quickly to instructions
■ work in role
■ use language and actions to convey situations, characters and emotions
■ use actions to convey situations, characters and emotions
■ comment constructively on drama in which they have participated.

CROSS-CURRICULAR LINKS

PSHE

Working co-operatively; following rules; setting and achieving simple goals; taking part in discussions.

RESOURCES AND LESSON ORGANIZATION

You will need a large space in which to work. Children work in pairs, changing partners regularly.

WHAT TO DO

Tell the children that you are going to ask them to do some instant performing. Explain that this could be acting out a scene, performing a mime or creating a freeze. Stress to the children that they will not have any time to prepare; that their performances must be given spontaneously on your command of *Go!*

Instruct the children to find a partner each and to stand together in a space. Tell them to act out a scene in which one of them is a shopkeeper and their partner is someone buying sweets in the shop. Allow two or three seconds for the children to select their roles and then give them the command to begin. Allow this scene to run for up to 30 seconds and then instruct the children to find new partners as quickly as they can.

Tell the children this time to perform a mime of two people juggling, giving the command *Go!* as soon as they have all found new partners. Allow this to continue for up to 30 seconds and then tell the children to find another new partner.

Give the pairs the scene of two people having an argument to create in a freeze. For this, give them a countdown from five and then the instruction *Freeze!* Take some time to move around the room briefly, viewing each of the freezes. Then ask the children to find new partners as quickly as possible.

Tell them to perform a mime of two people cheering on their favourite sports team. Allow a couple of seconds preparation time for this one and then give the instruction *Go!* Insist on silence during the mimes.

After about 30 seconds, ask the children to find another new partner and to act out a scene in which one of them is asking the other for directions. Allow two or three seconds for the children to select their roles and then *Go!* Let this scene to run for up to 30 seconds before instructing the children to stop.

Ask the children to gather together and rest. Encourage them to reflect on their work by asking: *What do you think you have learned from doing this activity?* (To work quickly and well with others.) *Why is that important?* (It helps us to co-operate and to use our imaginations.) *How could these skills benefit other areas of drama?* (Performances rely on teamwork and might require us to think and react quickly.)

ENGLISH

Listening and speaking to other people; sharing ideas and experiences; taking turns in speaking.

NOW OR LATER

■ Invite some of the children to show their freezes, mimes or improvisations to the rest of the class.

■ Repeat the activity using only freezes, mimes or improvisations.

■ Expand the improvisations to include additional characters.

CHARACTER IMPROVISATION

RESOURCES AND LESSON ORGANIZATION
You will need a large space in which to work. Children work in pairs.

WHAT TO DO
Tell the children that they are going to act out scenes as different characters. Ask them to find a partner to work with and to label themselves 'A' or 'B'. Explain that 'A' will be acting as a character and 'B' will be acting as someone speaking to that character. For example, if 'A' is a postwoman, 'B' could be someone who is having a large parcel delivered to them. Ask the children: *What other scenes could be acted out between characters and other people speaking to them?* (For example, doctor and patient; police officer and thief; shop assistant and customer; window cleaner and house owner.) Let them know that they can talk in these scenes, but remind them to move like their characters as well as speaking like them.

Call out characters from the following list: postman, hairdresser, police officer, teacher, doctor. Allow the children a few seconds to prepare their scene if necessary and ensure that they all understand what roles they are playing. After 'A' has acted as the character for a short while, tell the children to swap roles, instructing 'B's to act as that character and 'A's as someone speaking to them. The children should swap roles for each character given.

Advise the children that their swapped scenes can be in exactly the same setting or a different context entirely. Encourage them to think of interesting scenes where their characters would speak to each other. Nominate some partnerships with interesting, imaginative ideas to show their scenes to the rest of the class.

Finally, encourage the children to reflect on their work by asking: *What do you think you've learned from doing that activity? How could you improve your performances?* (By using our faces and bodies to express characters realistically; by planning our improvisations carefully; by responding well to what the other person is saying; by responding properly to who the other person is being.) *Which was the most difficult character to perform? Why? Which scene did you feel you acted well? Why?*

NOW OR LATER
■ See if the children can develop the improvisations into short scenes involving two or more characters.
■ Invite suggestions for characters from familiar stories that the children could improvise having conversations with each other.
■ Use the same process for historical figures meeting or having important discussions.

FIRST-LINE IMPROVISATIONS

RESOURCES AND LESSON ORGANIZATION
You will need a large work space; cards from photocopiable page 56. Children work together in small groups.

WHAT TO DO
Ask the children to form groups of up to six and tell them that each group is going to devise a short improvisation, or play, which they will perform to the rest of the

OBJECTIVES
To enable children to:
■ develop improvisation skills
■ create and sustain roles when working with others
■ use language and actions to convey characters
■ consider character development by reflecting on their own drama
■ comment constructively on drama in which they have participated.

CROSS-CURRICULAR LINKS
PSHE
Working co-operatively; listening to others; gaining self-confidence; setting and achieving goals.

ENGLISH
Speaking to different people; using appropriate language and intonation; sharing ideas.

OBJECTIVES
To enable children to:
■ create, sequence and develop scenes and events
■ work in role
■ present drama to others
■ create and sustain roles
■ evaluate performances.

CROSS-CURRICULAR
LINKS
PSHE
Developing interpersonal
skills; facing challenges;
contributing to group work;
gaining self-confidence.

ENGLISH
Listening to others; speaking
confidently and clearly;
responding appropriately to
others; sharing ideas and
experiences; evaluating ideas
in responding to drama.

class. Explain that each of these improvisations will have to begin with a specific line, given on a card and that their plays must then follow from the line they select.

Turn the cards face down and ask each group to select one. Do not allow groups to change their cards once their 'first lines' have been selected. Inform the children that they have a maximum of ten minutes to discuss, plan, prepare and rehearse their performances and encourage them to think about sequencing events realistically, developing and sustaining their roles and creating believable endings. Advise the children that their performances must not last longer than three minutes.

When all of the children understand what is expected of them and have begun their preparations, move quickly from group to group, giving support and resolving any difficulties. Give the children regular updates on the time remaining and, when the time limit has elapsed, designate an area of the room as the performance area and view each improvisation in turn.

Invite the children observing as an audience to make constructive comments after each presentation. Ask questions such as: *Was that performance realistic? Did you believe in the character and events? How well do you think it was presented? How could they have made it more interesting, realistic or effective? What do you feel was good about the play? Which characters did you find interesting or well portrayed?* Children who have just performed could also be asked for their assessment: *How did you think that went? Were you happy with what you achieved? Why? Why not? What would you change if you had the opportunity? What did you find the most difficult part of devising your performance?*

NOW OR LATER
■ Use the evaluations as a basis for children to refine and re-present their improvisations.
■ Invite the children to suggest alternative first lines and create new improvisations from them.
■ Ask the children to create additional scenes for their plays – either before or after the scene performed.
■ Ask the children to write up their plays in scripted form.
■ Use the same process for creating 'last-line improvisations', with more confident groups devising short plays that have to end on a specified closing line.

You can't bring that in here!

PERSON, PLACE, PROP

OBJECTIVES
To enable children to:
■ create and sustain roles
■ use language and actions to convey situations and characters
■ develop improvisation skills
■ present drama to others
■ comment constructively on drama in which they have participated
■ respond to performances.

RESOURCES AND LESSON ORGANIZATION   P.3/4
You will need a large work space; cards from photocopiable pages 57–9. Children work together in small groups, then take part in a whole-class discussion.

WHAT TO DO
Ask the children to form groups of four to six. Explain that they are going to plan and act out a scene, or short play, that they will create. Tell the children that each group will take one card from each of the 'person', 'place' and 'prop' piles, which are face down, and that they should then create a short improvisation based around those three elements.

Advise the children that their short plays can have any storyline, but that it must contain reference to the person, place and prop (object) on the cards they pick. Explain that each scene, or short play, must be no more than two minutes in length and that they will all be performed to the rest of the class, who will try to guess which cards were selected. Let them know that they will have only ten minutes from selecting their cards to discuss, plan and rehearse their short improvisations.

When all of the children understand what is expected of them, ask each group to take a card from each of the person, place and prop piles and to begin devising their improvisations. Make sure no one goes back to the piles to try to change a selection! Move quickly from group to group, ensuring that everyone is working co-operatively and effectively, and resolve any casting disputes. Whilst the children are planning and rehearsing, give regular updates on the time remaining and remind them that their improvisations should last no longer than two minutes.

When the time limit has elapsed, designate one area of the room as the performance area and ask each of the groups in turn to perform their improvisations. Remind the audience to remain silent whilst other groups are performing and, after each improvisation, lead the applause and a brief discussion. Ask the observers to comment on:

- what three elements they thought the play was based on
- how realistic the scene was
- how effective the acting was
- how well the improvisation was presented, for example could all the actors be seen and heard?

When all the groups have performed, ask the children to sit in a circle and reflect on the activity. Ask: *Did you enjoy that? Why? Why not? Which improvisation did you think was the best out of all of those seen?* (Try to dissuade children from nominating their own!) *What would you change about your own performances if you could do them again? What did you like about your own performances? What do you think this activity teaches you?* (To work together; to devise and sustain roles; to create realistic improvisations; how to perform to an audience; to watch and comment constructively on drama; to think about how we devise and perform scenes.)

NOW OR LATER
- Make your own additions to the person, place and prop cards.
- Invite the children to suggest additions for each element.
- Select a particular card yourself and ask all of the children to devise improvisations based on that subject.
- Ask the children to write up their improvisations as short playscripts.
- See if the children can write their own creative stories based around a particular person, place or prop.

MIMING TO NARRATION

RESOURCES AND LESSON ORGANIZATION
You will need a medium to large work space; the story on photocopiable pages 60 and 61. Children work in small groups and as a whole class.

WHAT TO DO
Ask the children to sit in a circle or in their classroom places. Read 'The three little pigs'. Discuss the content and structure of the story with the children exploring particularly the characters, events and settings. Clear a small space in one area of the room – this could be the 'play' corner or carpeted section – and inform the children that this is now the performance area. Explain that you are now going to read through the story again, but that this time some of the children will mime the actions of the characters in the story as you read it.

Select volunteers to act as the various characters (and scenery, objects, animals and so on) which represent the story. Allocate roles fairly and carefully. Position those

CROSS-CURRICULAR LINKS
PSHE
Working co-operatively; gaining self-confidence; taking part in discussions; setting and achieving goals.

ENGLISH
Listening to other people; speaking to different people; sharing ideas and experiences; taking part in group discussions.

OBJECTIVES
To enable children to:
- act out well-known stories
- explore familiar characters
- present drama and stories to others
- use language and actions to convey characters and emotions
- use actions to convey situations
- comment constructively on drama in which they have participated.

CROSS-CURRICULAR
LINKS
PSHE
Working co-operatively;
gaining self-confidence;
recognizing skills and
achievements; taking part in
discussions.

ENGLISH
Listening to adults and each
other; speaking to different
people; sharing experiences;
responding imaginatively to
familiar stories.

children representing scenery or objects in appropriate places in the performance area and ensure that the other children appreciate who or what these children represent. Ask the children representing characters to mime the actions of that character as they are related. Ensure that all of the children remember and understand that mime is action without words or sound.

If scene changes are required, select additional children to represent scenery, furniture or objects in other scenes and advise the children already in position that they will be replaced as and when required. When you have allocated roles to every child and have planned the scenery changes, explain that you will read the story again and that this time the children will perform mimes to represent the story in movement.

When all of the children understand what you want them to do, begin reading the story again. Read slowly, stopping as necessary to accommodate the mimed actions and to create scenes or settings. Assist the children by directing their participation, telling them when they are to move into the performance area and when to leave it. Continue until you have read the whole of the story and the children have mimed their representation of it.

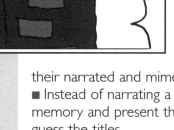

At this point they may want to repeat the exercise, with different volunteers taking on the roles of characters, objects and scenery. If you have time, this repetition could be ideally used to refine and improve the original performance and also for reducing your direction, allowing the children greater responsibility for their own entrances and exits.

When the exercise has been completed, thank and praise the children for their efforts. Lead a discussion, asking the children what they enjoyed about the activity, what they think they have learned from it and how they feel the skills gained could be applied to other areas of their school life.

NOW OR LATER

■ Rather than reading the story yourself, select a child to narrate whilst you organize and direct the 'actors'.
■ Apply the same method to a different story, poem, song or action rhyme.
■ Organize the children into small groups, allocate each group a different story or poem and ask them to present their narrated and mimed performances to the rest of the class.
■ Instead of narrating a story, ask the children to mime other familiar stories from memory and present these in small groups to the rest of the class for others to guess the titles.
■ Ask the children, working in small groups or as a whole class, to write their own story and to present these to an audience in the same manner.

ASK ME A QUESTION

OBJECTIVES
To enable children to:
■ explore familiar characters
■ respond to 'teacher in role'
to explore character
■ consider character motives
and issues
■ comment constructively
on drama.

RESOURCES AND LESSON ORGANIZATION

You will need a small to medium work space; a copy for each child of the story on photocopiable pages 62 and 63; an item of clothing as 'costume' (optional); paper; writing materials.

Children work as a whole class, then in small groups, then as a whole class again.

WHAT TO DO

Sit at the front of the classroom, or with the children in a circle. Read through 'Goldilocks and the three bears' with the children. Encourage the children to focus on the characters in the story by asking such questions as: *What sort of person is*

Goldilocks? Do you think she's good or naughty? Why? How do you think her mummy feels about Goldilocks? Why do you think Goldilocks disobeyed her mummy? How do you think the bears feel when they find Goldilocks in their house?

Now explain to the children that they are going to have the opportunity to ask Goldilocks some questions. *If you could ask Goldilocks something, what would you want to know?* When you have acknowledged several responses, organize the children into groups of up to six and tell them that you want them to prepare a list of questions to ask Goldilocks. Appoint a child in each group to write these questions down. Let them know they have about 15 minutes and should write a maximum of 5 questions.

When each group has prepared their questions, bring forward a chair and say: *I am now going to be Goldilocks and will answer the questions you have prepared for me.* (Although going into role is more about adopting an attitude, rather than 'becoming' another person, it may be useful for you to make the distinction between yourself and Goldilocks by putting on an appropriate item of clothing or costume at this point.)

Invite the children to ask their questions, selecting groups in turn. If the children find it difficult to control their questioning, or to take turns, come out of role and say: *I would like Goldilocks to have one question from each member of your group in turn. Can you do that?* Adopt your role again and respond as Goldilocks to each question asked, remaining in character regardless of the questions posed and repeating answers if necessary. Continue until all the questions have been asked and then come out of role again.

Encourage the children to reflect on the activity by asking: *What did you learn about Goldilocks that you didn't know before? Were there any other questions that you could have asked? Will knowing the answers make it easier to act as Goldilocks?* (Yes, because when we know and understand characters, we can act as them more realistically.)

NOW OR LATER

■ Repeat the process with other characters from the story, for example each of the three bears.
■ Repeat the process with other characters not mentioned in, but associated with, the story, for example Goldilocks's mum, her friends, the bears' friends.
■ Invite children to answer questions in role as characters from the story.
■ Ask the groups to record the answers in writing alongside their questions.
■ Ask the children in pairs to role-play an interview. One child could take on a character from the story, the other a newspaper reporter. These can then be written up as newspaper reports.
■ Decide as a class what punishment Goldilocks should receive for going into the bears' house.
■ Ask the children to write a letter from Goldilocks, apologizing to the three bears for her behaviour.

Section 5

CROSS-CURRICULAR LINKS
PSHE
Working co-operatively; taking part in discussions; listening to other people; exploring behaviour.

ENGLISH
Making plans and investigating; sharing ideas and experiences; speaking to different people; asking questions; taking turns in speaking.

First lines

You can't bring that in here.

Just what do you mean by that remark?

Don't look at me like that.

You'll never get that in there!

Are you as nervous as I am?

What was that?

What happened?

Who are you?

Name   Date

Person

alien

teacher

postman

cowboy

prison officer

ice-cream seller

bank robber

astronaut

Ready to go! **IDEAS FOR DRAMA**

Place

library

prison

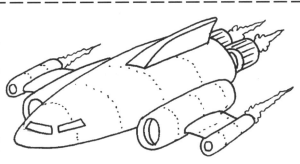

spaceship

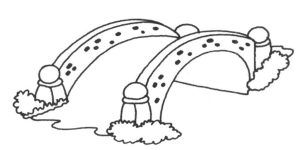

bridge

desert

school playground

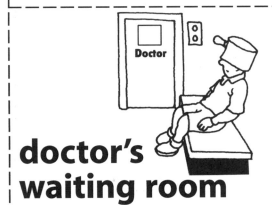

doctor's waiting room

fairground

Ready to go! IDEAS FOR DRAMA

Prop

ice-cream

bunch of keys

dictionary

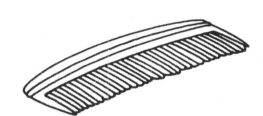

comb

pair of sunglasses

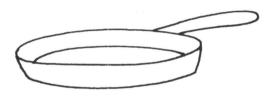

frying pan

orange

football

Ready to go! IDEAS FOR DRAMA

The three little pigs
(a traditional folk tale)

Once upon a time, three little pigs, Hammy, Tammy and Sammy, decided it was about time they left home and found their own place to live. So, the next day they packed up their belongings and some food, kissed their mother goodbye and left home. They walked until lunchtime, when they sat by the road, ate half their sandwiches and had a drink. The meal made them feel sleepy and, after a short nap, they set off again. After an hour or two, Hammy felt too tired to go any further.

"But we haven't got anywhere yet!" Sammy and Tammy said. "What are you going to do for a house?"

They were next to a field full of wheat that had just been cut. "I'll build a house out of straw," Hammy said. "Leave me here, it's a nice place for my new home."

Sammy and Tammy hugged their brother and carried on walking. Hammy set to work, gathering straw from the field, and built his house. When he finished, clouds covered the sky and the air was growing cold. He was beginning to get nervous, imagining he could see a dark hairy shadow in the wood. Suddenly Hammy wished he'd gone on with his brother and sister, but he was happy with his little house and soon settled himself inside.

Sammy and Tammy carried on walking, stopping to rest occasionally and eat more of their food. Much further down the road, Tammy was exhausted. "This is a very nice spot," she said. "I will build my house here."

"What will you build it from?" asked Sammy.

There was a pile of wood that a woodcutter had left, perfect for building a big strong house. "That wood," said Tammy, pointing to the large stack. Sammy and Tammy hugged and Sammy continued on his way. In no time at all Tammy had built her new home of sticks of wood, and she was very pleased with it. By this time the sky was beginning to get dark and Tammy was a little nervous, but she was happy with her little house and soon settled herself inside.

Sammy continued walking until he could go no further. He noticed a brick factory at the side of the road and decided to build his house right there. He bought enough bricks and cement and set about building his new home. By the time he had finished, the sky was dark and it was night. He became very nervous then, wishing he'd stayed with his brother or sister, but he was happy with his little house and soon settled himself inside.

A little while later, at Hammy's house, there came a tapping at the door which woke Hammy from his deep sleep. "Little pig, little pig, let me come in," a voice said.

Hammy was terrified. Now he knew what the shadow in the wood had been – a wolf! "You're not coming in here, not by the hair on my chinny-chin-chin," he said in his most grown-up voice.

"Then I'll huff and I'll puff and I'll blow your house down!" the wolf snarled. So the wolf huffed and he puffed and Hammy's house collapsed to the ground in a heap of straw. Hammy leapt out of the window and ran as fast as his legs could carry him to his sister's house.

Hammy and Tammy were huddled together in fear when suddenly a gentle tapping could be heard at her door. "Little pig, little pig, let me come in," a voice said softly. "I'm lonely and hungry. I want a bite to eat."

Their little hearts gave a thump. "It's the wolf!" Hammy cried.

Tammy put on her most brave voice and said "Wolf! You don't fool me! You're not coming in, not by the hair on my chinny-chin-chin!"

"Then I'll huff and I'll puff and I'll blow your house down!" the wolf snarled. And he huffed and he puffed and Tammy's house collapsed to the ground in a heap of sticks. As the wolf was huffing and puffing, Hammy and Tammy leapt out of the window and ran as fast as their legs

could carry them to their brother's house.

Hammy, Tammy and Sammy were huddled together in terror when suddenly the tapping sound came again, this time at Sammy's door. "I'm a friend of your brother and sister," he called. "Little pig, little pig, let me come in."

"It's the wolf!" cried Hammy and Tammy together.

"You don't fool me, wolf, my sister and brother are here and you're not coming in, not by the hair on my chinny-chin-chin!" Sammy shouted.

"Then I'll huff and I'll puff and I'll blow your house down!" the wolf snarled. He drew a deep breath and huffed and puffed as hard as he could. The house didn't move. The wolf huffed and he puffed again with all his might, but still the house stood firm because it was built of bricks. The wolf huffed and puffed again and again, but only the doors and windows rattled. In a towering rage, the wolf leapt up onto the roof and began to climb down the chimney. But Sammy knew what he was up to and quickly put a huge pot of water on the fire to boil. Instead of landing in the fireplace, ready to eat them, the wolf fell into the big pot and was boiled up.

How happy the three little pigs were to be rid of the nasty old wolf. Safe and sound, in Sammy's house built of bricks, they all lived together happily ever after.

Goldilocks and the three bears

Once upon a time, three bears lived in a house in the woods. They were called Little Bear, Middle Bear and Big Bear. Their house, which they kept very neat and tidy, was full of just the right-sized things – bowls, cups, spoons, chairs, beds – anything you could think of.

One morning, it was Big Bear's turn to make the breakfast. He ladled the porridge into the bowls, just the right amount in each. But when the bears sat down to eat, the porridge was far too hot. They decided to go for a walk while it cooled.

Two minutes after they had set off, who should come past their house but a little girl called Goldilocks. Goldilocks was a naughty child who always did exactly what she wanted. She shouldn't even have been in the woods (her mummy had sent her to the shop to buy some milk). But there she was and she knew the bears were out walking. She tried the door. It wasn't locked, so in she went.

Goldilocks spied what was on the table. "Porridge!" She licked her lips. "My favourite!" She tried the porridge in Big Bear's bowl first. "Ow!" she cried. "That's far too hot."

She spat it out. Next she tried the porridge in Middle Bear's bowl. "Ugh!" she said. "That's too cold!" She spat that out too. Lastly, she tried the porridge in Little Bear's bowl. "Mmm," she said. "That's just right!" And she gobbled it all up.

Then, because she needed a rest after all her wandering about in the woods, Goldilocks tried Big Bear's chair. "That's far too hard," she said. "No good to me." Then she sat in Middle Bear's chair. "That's much too soft," she said. "Very uncomfortable." Finally, she tried Little Bear's chair. "Just right," she said happily. But as she made herself more comfortable, the chair collapsed and completely broke apart!

Goldilocks was determined to have a rest, however, so upstairs she went and opened the bedroom door. First she tried Big Bear's bed, but it was too lumpy. Next she tried Middle Bear's bed, but that was too hard and uncomfortable. Then she tried Little Bear's bed. It was perfect! Without even taking off her shoes, Goldilocks tucked herself in and went straight to sleep.

Ready to go! IDEAS FOR DRAMA

Meanwhile, the bears returned home from their walk. They hung their coats up neatly and went to eat their porridge. Except, except…

"Who's been eating my porridge?" Big Bear growled. "They've even left the spoon in it."

"And who's been eating my porridge?" asked Middle Bear.

"And who's been eating my porridge, and eaten it all up?" Little Bear sobbed. The three bears looked about. Someone had been in their house without permission and they didn't like that one little bit.

"Who's been sitting in my chair," Big Bear growled, "and thrown my cushion onto the floor?"

"Who's been sitting in my chair," growled Middle Bear, "and made my cushion all squashed?"

"Who's been sitting in my chair?" sobbed Little Bear, "They've broken it all up!" And he cried even louder.

"Sshh," Big Bear said. "What's that noise?" The three bears listened.

"It's someone snoring," said Middle Bear. The three bears looked at each other.

"Whoever it is, they're still here!" Little Bear said. The three bears crept upstairs. They went into the bedroom. "Who's been lying on my bed?" Big Bear growled. "My bed covers are all creased!"

"Who's been lying on my bed?" grumbled Middle Bear. "The pillows are all messed up!"

"Who's been lying on my bed?" squeaked Little Bear. "And look, they're still lying in it!" he shouted.

Little Bear's shrill voice woke Goldilocks up with a start. She took one look at the bears standing in a row along one side of the bed, jumped out of the other side, ran through the door, down the stairs and out of the house as fast as her legs would carry her, trampling all over the flowers planted neatly in the garden as she went.

"How dare she sleep in my bed!" exclaimed Little Bear.

"She's trampled all over the flowers!" grumbled Middle Bear.

"She hasn't even closed the gate!" moaned Big Bear.

And they went about putting their house in order again.

What happened to Goldilocks no one knows. Maybe her mother just scolded her for not bringing the milk. Or maybe she did something worse, when she found out where Goldilocks had been and what she had really been up to!

 **NATIONAL STANDARDS FOR KEY SKILLS**

The grid below will help you to identify which activities can be used to develop specific key skills, and enable you to check on the overall balance of skill development in your teaching programme. These skills are based on the QCA's National Standards for Key Skills (and the revised orders for the English curriculum).

SKILLS DEVELOPED IN SECTIONS	1	2	3	4	5
Working positively with others	✔	✔	✔	✔	✔
Following specific instructions	✔	✔	✔	✔	✔
Developing communication skills	✔	✔	✔	✔	✔
Using actions to convey situations, characters and emotions		✔	✔	✔	✔
Responding as themselves in a fictional setting		✔	✔	✔	✔
Creating and sustaining roles individually		✔	✔	✔	✔
Creating and sustaining roles when working with others		✔	✔	✔	✔
Using language to convey situations, characters and emotions			✔	✔	✔
Presenting drama to others			✔	✔	✔
Improvising and working in role			✔	✔	✔
Developing scenes, events or incidents				✔	✔
Using conventions to explore characters					✔
Commenting constructively on drama in which they have participated		✔	✔	✔	✔
Commenting constructively on drama they have watched				✔	✔